HUNTING

TRUTH

Chris Harman

Cover and Illustrations By: Julie Harman Dovan

ISBN 978-1-63885-525-5 (Paperback)
ISBN 978-1-63885-526-2 (Digital)

All scripture quotations were taken from the King James
Version of the Holy Bible unless otherwise stated.

Covenant Books
11661 Hwy 707
Murrells Inlet, SC 29576
www.covenantbooks.com

To my children and my family, may this book encourage you in God's word and draw you closer to the Lord Jesus Christ that your joy may be full.

TABLE OF CONTENTS

Acknowledgments vii

Introduction.. ix

1. Lessons in Nature..1

2. The Family 17

3. The Heart of a Bird Dog...39

4. The Shotgun...61

5. The Powers of the Air 79

6. The Hoot Owl...95

7. Maddie's Broken Leg...113

8. Rough Terrain..129

9. Comradery...149

10. Coming Home..167

ACKNOWLEDGMENTS

Special thanks, to Rebecca, my lovely wife, who has always been by my side and encouraged me to move forward and continue writing. To my sister, Julie Harman Dovan, for the artwork on the cover and chapter sketches. To my parents, Chris and Ginny Harman, for their support through this journey. To Wanda Combs, for pre-editing the manuscript. To Rev. James Cockram, Susan Brown, and the many mentors that God has so graciously surrounded me with. To New Haven Baptist Church for the encouragement as well as the privilege to teach and to serve. Most of all, to the God of all creation, my Blessed Savior, may He use this book to further the gospel of Jesus Christ and bring honor and glory to His name.

INTRODUCTION

One late October afternoon while grouse hunting in the mountains of Virginia, I watched my young Brittany bird dog, Maddie, work through a briar thicket. As she caught the scent of a grouse, I could see her excitement overflowing, her bobbed tail wagging faster back and forth. I could see her determination while she struggled to move through the thick briars; the tip of her tail is now stained with blood. It is Maddie's desire to find and point a bird, pleasing her master. As I observed Maddie, I thought, *What if I could serve my Master, the Lord Jesus Christ, like she serves me? What if I could point others not to a bird, but to Jesus Christ through teaching His simple truths that they might serve Him as well?*

I realize God can reveal His blessed truths through a simple grouse hunt. As we journey through the mountains, we can see a small glimpse into the mind of our Creator.

Before we can serve the Creator, we must first acknowledge that He is the Creator of all things. He makes Himself known through creation in the "Lessons in Nature." This moves man to hunt for deeper truths and find out that our Creator is a loving God who loved us enough to come to earth and die on a Roman cross to pay for the sins of the world. When we believe in Him, He gives us the power to become the sons of God and welcomes us into His family. When we enter into "The Family" of God. "Old things are passed away; behold, all things become new" (2 Cor. 5:17). We are a new creation in Christ Jesus. With our new heart, our service is no longer to ourselves but to our Lord with "The Heart of a Bird Dog."

We serve our God through the power of the Holy Spirit, and His written word. Just like "The Shotgun," His word is our trusted weapon in the battle against "The Powers of the Air." Many times, we will get off track, not knowing which way to turn; but we find comfort, knowing that just like calling the "Hoot Owl," we can call to our Savior at any time. We learn from "Maddie's Broken Leg," which was once a hindrance but now has been put behind her. Our Lord forgives our past sins, so we need to put them behind us, and when others sin against us, we must forgive and likewise put them in the past, looking forward to that blessed hope.

Like pilgrims, we are just passing through. Our citizenship is not of this world but of one to come. Along the way, we will wander through "Rough Terrain." Though it may seem hopeless at times, our Savior will be with us all the way. He also brings those into our lives who help and encourage us, forming a special "Comradery." In "Coming Home" ultimately, we long for the day when we see our Savior face-to-face and hear those blessed words, "Well done, thy good and faithful servant. Welcome home."

LESSONS IN NATURE

"Are you ready to go, Maddie ole girl?"

Maddie is riding shotgun today. She sits up straight and proud as she looks out the window. She turns her head to glance at me over her shoulder. Those wiry-haired ears perk up and stand at attention. With her mouth open and her tongue hanging out, she appears to be grinning from ear to ear. It's as if she cannot contain the excitement any longer. Summertime has passed, and autumn is in full swing. October is coming to an end. Grouse season is just beginning.

We pull over on the side of an old logging road. Maddie begins to whimper. She just can't stand it any longer. Her excitement is boiling over, and she is ready to go.

"Whoa, Maddie," I command as I get out of the truck and put the electronic collar on her neck. "Break!"

She dives out of the truck and hits the ground, running wide open, never missing a beat. She sprints down the road almost out of sight, then spins around and races back up the hill. Stretching out in full stride, she changes leads like a thoroughbred racing at Churchill Downs. She then swings up over the next ridge and works back down the hill through the saplings like a slalom skier. Finally, after several minutes, she seems to have burned off enough energy to begin hunting.

With my shotgun in hand and Maddie in the lead, we begin to hike up the side of the mountain. I cannot help but notice the beauty around me. The remaining autumn leaves with their vibrant colors catch my attention. As we move higher up the mountain, I can now see the majestic Blue Ridge Mountains surrounding me. The blue and purple hue of the mountains mingling with fluorescent orange, red, and yellow is absolutely breathtaking. The sky is a crisp blue with the streak of a violet cloud passing by, as if an artist's brushstroke painted it on a canvas. I can hear a small stream trickling below; the birds chirping; a gray squirrel barking in the distance; and a few katydids left over from summer, making up a beautiful symphony. I enjoy hunting grouse especially this time of year. Yes, I like to kill a few birds as much as the next guy, but just getting out and enjoying the scenery is rewarding enough. I walk a short distance, and then I have to stop, step back, and look, taking it all in. It is amazing to me when observing nature that there are so many lessons to be learned.

I am reminded of the words David penned in Psalm 8:3, "When I consider thy heavens, the work of thy fingers, the moon and the stars, which thou hast ordained." When I look around and see the marvelous creation, I have to think as David did: how great God is, yet I am so small. "All things were made by Him (Jesus Christ the son of God); and without Him was not anything made that was made" (John 1:3). God created the heavens and the earth and everything in them. According to the Bible, everything was made by Him in six literal days. We are so intricately and wonderfully made, created for His glory; and we, being His creation, are accountable to Him.

There are those who don't believe in the Creator. In fact, they believe that somehow millions of years ago there was a big bang and everything evolved from there. By believing this theory, man has made himself a god. Without God, he becomes the superior being. He is the captain of his domain and the lord of his soul and can do as he pleases. He is accountable to no one. Why does man accept something that was only a theory as fact? So he would no longer be accountable to God. Man can then do his own will, what feels good and anything his heart desires, and karma or fate will deal with the consequences. If we are created by an Almighty God who sees all things and knows all things, then we are held accountable by the Creator for the things we think about, the words we say to one another, and the actions we take in life. All of those things would ultimately be judged by Him. That takes all the fun out of doing whatever feels right, doesn't it?

Seeing God's creation reminds me of Romans 1:19–20:

> Because that which may be known of God is manifest in them; for God hath shewed it unto them. For the invisible things of Him from the creation of the world are clearly seen, being understood by the things that are made, even His eternal power and Godhead; so that they are without excuse.

In other words, whether you believe you evolved from an ape or you believe you were created by the Almighty God, the Bible says we will all stand before Him one day; and because of His great creation, we will not be able to say, "I didn't know." No, you are without excuse.

Off in the distance I hear the sound of Canadian geese. I stop to watch them fly through the valley below. I wonder who taught them to fly south for the winter. How do they know to fly in a V shape? Who told them that flying in this pattern makes them more aerodynamic so they use less energy as they travel hundreds of miles? Who taught Maddie how to hunt birds and to point when she catches the warm scent of a grouse or quail? These are instincts programmed by their very designer, the Creator.

What about you? How about that little voice called a conscience that nags you when you do wrong or when you wake up in the middle of the night and wonder, *Is there really a god? Are heaven and hell real? And if they are, in which of these will I spend eternity? Why am I here? What is my purpose in life?* These are things God has programmed in us. That is what is meant when it says, "That which may be known of God is manifest in them." When I look at the many minute details of the human body, the rising and setting of the sun and moon, and even the spiderweb that was so masterfully weaved (and which I had just walked through and got stuck to my face. Man, I hate that), I know everything has a purpose and, by design, works perfectly together. I can see through nature that everything didn't just fall into place after a big bang but was thoughtfully and carefully designed and formed by the Almighty Creator, the God of the universe.

Let's suppose everything did just evolve, and let's suppose there is no creator. What is your purpose? Why are you here? And what do you hope to accomplish? Think about it. You are born, you live your life here on this earth, you die, and that's it! What was your purpose? Without God, we aimlessly wander through life with our purpose to fulfill the lust and desires of our own hearts. Sure, there are those who do good works and help others, maybe to the point of changing one's life for the better; but without God, nothing lasts forever and your purpose is only temporary. Without God, many take on the lifestyle of the animal kingdom, in which they have the mentality to gain all they can in life; to lie, cheat, and steal their way to the top. If they don't get caught, it's all fair game because in the animal kingdom, the strong survive and the weak die. Remember there is no creator and no God that knows all things, and you can't be held accountable for your sins. With no creator, it seems we enjoy ourselves for a while, and that's it. We die, and we are forgotten. I don't know about you, but that doesn't sound like much of a purpose to me. No wonder people walk around with long faces. They have nothing to look forward to, and they have no true joy or purpose.

I have come out against evolution and in favor of creation. Maybe you don't believe in it. I can understand your doubt. I mean I am telling you to believe something that seems impossible. Needless to say, I wasn't there at creation nor was anyone else. All I have is the Holy Bible, and though it does give some detail about how some things were made, it does take faith to believe in creation. However, I am amazed how a scientist who believes in evolution can be walking along, pick up a rock, study it for a few seconds, exclaim "3.7 million years old," drop it, and continue on his way. May I ask a dumb question? Was he there when that rock was made? What does he have to prove his theory? Well, of course, it takes faith. But faith in what?

I base my faith on the Bible and on the creation that I can see. On what do you base your faith? Charles Darwin was born in 1809, several thousand years after the book of Genesis was written. He based his theory on similarities of species. I have often wondered,

4

How do you get the big bang theory that happened millions or billions of years ago from similarities? Now that takes faith. Many don't believe in a creator because they can't see the creator.

As Maddie and I move higher up the mountain, the wind begins to pick up. I have to ask the question, Have you ever seen the wind? Of course not. So how do you know it's there? You cannot see the wind; but you can see, hear, or feel the effects. You can see the trees swaying, you can hear as it blows through the leaves and branches, and you can feel it on your skin. I have never seen God. I have never seen Jesus Christ. But when I put my faith in Him and accepted Him as my personal Savior, I felt the effects because He changed my life completely. You may question my belief of creation and salvation, but you cannot question the effects it has brought to my life. If the Bible tells me that He can make me a new creature, I believe it because I have seen and experienced the change and the true joy the Bible teaches.

Let me introduce you to my God, the God of the Bible and the one I have grown to love and serve throughout my life. Trust me. From the looks of it, you have nothing to lose. The God of the Bible is first of all omniscient, which means all-knowing. Everything that you think, see, or say He knows. He knows when and also before you think, see, or say something. He is omnipresent, which means He is everywhere all the time. David says in Psalm 139:8, "If I ascend up into heaven, thou art there: if I make my bed in hell, behold, thou art there." God is omnipotent, meaning He is all-powerful. There is nothing He cannot accomplish. He is also loving, and He is holy. I can't help but to cringe when I hear people refer to God as the man upstairs or the big guy. He is Almighty God. He is to be reverenced. He is righteous, without sin, and perfect in every way. He is the just judge, and in Him, there is no corruption. The question is, What does that mean to you? Again, what is your purpose? Or maybe you ask yourself, What is it all about? I'm glad you finally asked!

In the beginning, God created the heavens and the earth. We get that from the book of Genesis in the first chapter. After everything was created, God created Adam, who would manage and take care of everything in the Garden of Eden. In addition to caring for things in the garden, Adam also had fellowship with God, an actual relationship where he talked with God. Imagine a relationship with your father or mother, your children, or maybe even a best friend. We see that in Genesis 3:8 when they heard God walking in the cool of the day. God was actually coming down to talk with Adam and Eve, maybe to ask them how their day was, to tell them some truth about Himself or just to let them know that He loved them. You see, that is our purpose: to serve God and also to have a personal relationship with the very One who created us.

Adam and Eve had that personal relationship with God, and He desires that you and I also have a relationship with Him. But something happened in the Garden of Eden. Adam and Eve disobeyed God and ate of the fruit of the tree of the knowledge of good and evil, the fruit of the tree God commanded them not to eat. They sinned against God, the one who created them, the one who came to fellowship with them in the cool of the day, the one who loved them. The sin of Adam and Eve blocked that fellowship, destroying the relationship they had with God. They were no longer perfect, and nothing that is imperfect can be in the presence of a perfect and Holy God. Sin put a wall between God and man and destroyed the purpose God created us for to begin with. Because of their sin, a sin nature has been passed on from generation to generation down to you and me. Adam and Eve were held accountable for their sin and were now faced with the death penalty. We all likewise face this same death penalty. Paul tells us in Romans 5:12, "Wherefore, as by one man sin entered into the world, and death by sin; and so death passed upon all men, for that all have sinned." He writes in Romans 3:23, "For all have sinned, and come short of the glory of God." Finally, he states in Romans 3:10, "As it is written, There is none righteous, no, not one." So maybe you are thinking, What does that mean to me? Is God as a tyrant sitting in heaven, watching everything we do and waiting to destroy all of us because we have sinned against Him?

Let's go back and look at God again. Many believe God is love and that He is full of grace and mercy, and if you believe that, you are exactly right. So how can a loving God cast His creation into the lake of fire? I'm sure you can probably honestly say in your heart, "I've never killed anyone. I do my best. I have just made a few mistakes." In James 2:10, we read, "For whosoever shall keep the whole law, and yet offend in one point, he is guilty of all." So then, according to the scripture, you are still a sinner! As we said before, God is love and He is full of mercy and grace. But He is also holy, righteous, and just.

Think about this, suppose someone robbed you at gunpoint and stole a large sum of money. He was later arrested and stood before the judge. The judge ordered the robber to return the money, plus interest, and also serve time for the crime he committed. The robber pleaded with the judge that he could not repay the money and had family to support. The judge had compassion, and out of the love of his heart, he pardoned the robber and told him to "Go in peace." Has justice been served? Of course not. This man has walked away a free man, the debt has not been paid, and you don't have your money. There was no justice! Now suppose that judge handed down the same sentence, and the man pleaded with the judge. But this time the judge, out of the love of his heart, says to the robber, "I will pay the debt you owe, and I will serve the sentence myself. Go in peace." We not only see love and mercy, but also justice. God, being just, likewise cannot let sin go unpunished. He demands justice. The debt of sin, which is death, must be paid. "For the wages of sin is death" (Rom. 6:23). This is not a physical death as Hebrews 9:27 speaks of: "And as it is appointed unto men once to die, but after this the judgment." We see this physical death every day. We all will face this physical death sooner or later. Remember there are two sure things in this world, and those things are death and taxes. The death in Romans 6:23 is a spiritual death, meaning eternal separation from God and eternal darkness, also known as the place called hell, where the Bible says there is weeping, wailing, and gnashing of teeth and where fire and brimstone burn forever and ever and can never be quenched.

As awful as that sounds, I have good news! It's called the gospel of Jesus Christ! Remember the judge who substituted himself for the robber? God likewise substituted Himself in the person Jesus Christ. Paul writes in Romans 6:23, "For the wages of sin is death; *but* the gift of God is eternal life through Jesus Christ our Lord." John 3:16, probably the most well-known verse in the Bible, proclaims, "For God so loved the world, that He gave His only begotten Son, that whosoever believeth in Him should not perish, but have everlasting life."

To further explain this as simple as I know how, I want to use the three crosses of Calvary. In the gospel of Matthew 27:38, we read, "Then were there two thieves crucified with Him [Jesus], one on the right hand, and another on the left." As Jesus hung upon that cross, we see He was in the middle with a thief on each side. We are reminded of these three crosses as we travel up and down the interstates in America. Every few miles, you will see the three crosses off to the side of the road. These crosses represent our Lord Jesus Christ as He was hung on a cross between two thieves. I have to ask myself, Where is my cross? You and I have sinned against a holy God and have fallen far short of His glory. I certainly deserve no less than a cross of my own. So why aren't there four of them? It is because my cross and yours is in the middle. The wages of sin is death, and for justice to be served, each of us must die both physically and spiritually. The fact is, Jesus never sinned. Therefore, He didn't deserve to die, so that was not His cross. The cross that Jesus hung upon was mine and yours. God substituted His only son in our place.

Looking at the judge we talked about earlier. "For he hath made him to be sin for us, who knew no sin; that we might be made the righteousness of God in him" (2 Cor. 5:21). Jesus Christ, the perfect Lamb of God, the one who never sinned, paid for our sins. He was falsely accused and beaten with a cat-o'-nine-tails, which is a leather strap with nine branches, each having metal fragments designed to rip the skin on contact. They plucked out His beard, slapped Him numerous times across the face, and beat Him beyond recognition. They later placed a crown of thorns on His head, mocked Him, and spit in His face. He was then made to carry His cross up the hill of Calvary, and when He had no more energy and couldn't bear His cross any longer, someone else had to help Him. When they climbed the hill to the destination, they drove spikes through His wrists and through His feet and hung Him on that cross.

Why didn't He come down from that cross? He was the son of God. He had the power to call for His angels and destroy us all. But He willingly suffered; bled; and died for our sins, the sins of the world.

> For God so loved the world, that he gave (or substituted) his only begotten Son, (on that cross, in our place) that whosoever believeth in him should not perish, but have everlasting life. (John 3:16)

Notice why God gave His son Jesus to willingly hang on that cross. It is because He loves us and because He desires a relationship with you and me today. "When Jesus therefore had received the vinegar, he said, It is finished: and he bowed his head, and gave up the ghost" (John 19:30). It is finished! The price has been paid. The work has been done. Now we can have forgiveness of our sins, but He didn't just die, He arose from the grave on the third day giving us eternal life, and now we can have a relationship with Jesus Christ, our living savior, our Creator, the very one who made this gorgeous scenery.

So you ask yourself, What now? Are my sins forgiven, and that's it? Do I need to do something? In Romans 6:23, it is written, "For the wages of sin is death; but the 'gift' of God is eternal life through Jesus Christ our Lord." John 3:16 says that "whosoever believeth in him [receives that gift] should not perish, but have everlasting life." Jesus Christ has done the work. Remember He said, "It is finished," but He did it as a gift for you and me. Therefore, we have a choice to make: to receive or reject the gift. That brings us back to the other two crosses. Jesus hung on the middle cross as a substitute for you and me. I believe the other two crosses are examples of the choices we have to make.

I'm sure you have heard of the broad road and the narrow road: these are two choices. The two thieves each had to make a choice, and they made very different choices.

> Then were there two thieves crucified with him, one on the right hand, and another on the left. And they that passed by reviled him, wag-

ging their heads, and saying, thou that destroyest
the temple, and buildest it in three days, save thyself. If thou be the Son of God, come down from
the cross. Likewise also the chief priests mocking
him, with the scribes and elders, said, He saved
others; himself he cannot save. If he be the King
of Israel, let him now come down from the cross,
and we will believe him. He trusted in God; let
him deliver him now, if he will have him: for
he said, I am the Son of God. The thieves also,
which were crucified with him, cast the same in
his teeth. (Matt. 27:38–44)

In other words, as the people mocked Jesus, the thieves also
mocked Jesus, even though they faced certain death. They also had
spikes run through their wrists and hung from their own crosses.
They were gasping for every breath, helpless, hopeless. These men
were rightly suffering for the crime they had committed. As they
were facing certain death, we also face certain death. We are hopeless
and helpless. The thieves both chose to reject the Lord Jesus Christ.
The story continues in Luke 23:39–42:

> And one of the malefactors which were
> hanged railed on him, saying, "If thou be Christ,
> save thyself and us." But the other answering
> rebuked him, saying, "Dost not thou fear God,
> seeing thou art in the same condemnation? And
> we indeed justly; for we receive the due reward
> of our deeds: but this man hath done nothing
> amiss. And he said unto Jesus, Lord, remember
> me when thou comest into thy kingdom."

The thief on the left continues mocking Christ and will soon
face the judgment of God, because there was never a change in his
heart. He continues mocking Jesus until he can no longer speak,
but something happens to the thief on the right. There is a change

of heart. As he hangs on that cross, he realizes he is getting what he deserves. He also realizes he will soon face God's judgment. He then turns to Jesus as he pulls himself up to gasp for another breath and says, "Lord, remember me when you come into your kingdom."

I don't know if Jesus said something to this thief. If He did, it wasn't recorded. It may have been the way Jesus handled Himself through the whole crucifixion, or could it be that the thief remembered his father or mother teaching him as a young child that God would send a Savior to die for the sins of the world? Maybe he remembered his mother pleading with him years earlier, "Son, please follow after God. Seek His will for your life." Yet he turned to a life of self-sufficiency, replying, "I don't need God in my life. I'll do it my way." Now he has time to reflect on the choices he has made. He has time to think and nowhere else to turn. Sometimes God puts us in that same position as well. Maybe it's in a hospital bed or somewhere else where you can only look up. At this point, you have time to think about all the mistakes and failures in your life. I know of many people who trusted Jesus Christ as their personal savior on their deathbed, just like the thief on the cross. I would consider that a blessing from God. Not everyone gets that same opportunity.

Going back to the thief, I don't know what changed his mind, but I do know that he sees Jesus for who He is, the very Son of God who came to take away the sin of the world. Here is a man who has lived a hard life. He has made a mess of things. He is one that many have looked down on. He is a sinner with a capital *S*, but in the very next verse, verse 43, we read, "And Jesus said unto him, 'Verily I say unto thee, today shalt thou be with me in paradise." Forgiven! Saved! By the grace of God, this man deserved eternal judgment, torment in the lake of fire for eternity, but God in His mercy withheld that judgment and didn't give him what he deserved. At the same time, He showed him grace, giving him something he didn't deserve: eternal life and a home in paradise. How would you like to have salvation? All you have to do is put your faith and trust in Jesus Christ and accept the gift that He has given you even today.

The first thing we need to notice is that the thief didn't go back and try to do any good deeds. He didn't try to work or earn his way to heaven or attempt to find favor with God. Maybe you are thinking, *Well, I thought only the good people went to heaven.* Maybe you are trying to earn your way or to find favor with God. I want to show you a few verses in the Bible. In Isaiah 64:6a, we read, "But we are all as an unclean thing, and all our righteousnesses are as filthy rags." In Ephesians 2:8–9, it is written, "For by grace are ye saved through faith; and that not of yourselves: it is the gift of God: Not of works, lest any man should boast." The Bible tells us plainly that salvation is a gift and cannot be earned, no matter what we do, because we are all sinners. Good works are an outward evidence of salvation, not a means of salvation. The Bible talks about fruit trees. Jesus tells us in Matthew 7:17–18, "Even so every good tree bringeth forth good fruit; but a corrupt tree bringeth forth evil fruit. A good tree cannot bring forth evil fruit, neither can a corrupt tree bring forth good fruit." We are known by our fruits, and without Jesus Christ as Savior, you and I are corrupt trees with thorns that produce crab apples. We cannot bring forth good fruit or good works, apart from the power of our savior Jesus Christ.

The second thing we see is that the thief never went to see a priest. He was never sprinkled, and he did no rituals of any kind. He wasn't even baptized. Baptism is a public showing of the believer that he or she has trusted Jesus Christ as his or her personal Savior and has committed to follow Him. It is a picture of the death, burial, and resurrection and identifies the believer with Jesus Christ. It is, in fact, the first command for the believer once he or she has professed Jesus Christ as Savior. But it does not have anything to do with salvation. The thief did not take Communion or observe the Lord's Supper, although we are commanded as believers to observe the Lord's Communion, but only to remember what Jesus Christ did for us on the cross of Calvary and to show the Lord's death until He comes again. If any of these things had to be done for salvation, then Jesus could not have told the thief those wonderful and comforting words, "Today thou shalt be with me in paradise."

As they hung on their crosses, both thieves could see Jesus out of the corner of their eye, and as they looked upon Him, they had to answer the question, "Who is he?" and make the choice, "What do I do with him?" Jesus said in John 14:6, "I am the way, the truth, and the life: no man cometh unto the Father, but by me." By choosing Jesus Christ, the one thief entered into paradise, into the very presence of our Lord, and will be in His presence for all eternity.

Looking over these mountains, seeing the beauty of creation and hearing the symphony of the forest, it is comforting to know that the very Creator, the one that made it all, loved you and me enough to leave heaven's glory and come down to this earth to suffer, bleed, and die on a cross to pay for our sins so that we can be saved from our sins and have eternal life. Would you like to have that comfort and peace in your heart? Would you like to be saved from your sins and have that personal relationship with Him today? If so, you are at the crossroads. You are just like those two thieves. You are looking at Jesus out of the corner of your eye, and you have to make a choice. So the question is, What will you do with Jesus? Maybe the Lord has convicted your heart. Could it be that you have been unsure about salvation and you didn't know how to be saved? Salvation begins in the heart. So if you have truly believed in your heart that Jesus died on the cross to pay for your sins and that he arose from the grave on the third day, you can go to the Lord Jesus Christ right now and pray something like this:

> Lord, I have sinned against you, and I know that I am a sinner. I realize the punishment for sin is eternal separation from God and torment in the lake of fire, and I know that is what I deserve. But I believe that Jesus Christ died on that cross to pay for my sin and that He arose victorious from the grave on the third day, and I want to accept that gift of salvation. Please come into my heart and save me by your grace. Amen.

If you have truly believed in your heart and prayed that prayer, then you have become a child of God. The Bible says in Romans 10:9–10,

> That if thou shalt confess with thy mouth the Lord Jesus, and shalt believe in thine heart that God hath raised him from the dead, thou shalt be saved. For with the heart man believeth unto righteousness; and with the mouth confession is made unto salvation.

Verse 13 continues, "For whosoever shall call upon the name of the Lord shall be saved." Also in John 1:12, we read, "But as many as received him, to them gave he power to become the sons of God, even to them that believe on his name." If you have trusted Jesus Christ as your Savior, not only has He saved you but also you are now one of His children. You now have a new purpose no longer to yourself but to serve your Father in heaven.

As I try to comprehend the vast beauty around me, I am reminded, whether you are looking out over the mountains, the ocean, or the rolling hills, no matter where you are, you too can have that comfort knowing that a far greater beauty and a far greater place awaits us when one day we see our Savior face-to-face. Jesus said in John 14:2b–3, "I go to prepare a place for you. And if I go and prepare a place for you, I will come again, and receive you unto myself; that where I am, there ye may be also." Until then, we can only imagine the beauty of the place He has gone to prepare for you and me.

THE FAMILY

In 1969, I was born into the Harman family. In 1980, after struggling for several months with the thoughts of heaven and hell and where I would spend eternity after I died, a preacher by the name of Robert Blackwell sat down with me on the front pew of a little white country church just off the Blue Ridge Parkway and showed me from the Bible that I was a sinner and without hope. He also showed me that Jesus Christ came and died on the cross to pay for my sins. I realized I was heading in the wrong direction and that I needed a Savior, so by faith, I received the gift of salvation, and I was born into the family of God.

One cool, dark night a man by the name of Nicodemus came to Jesus. He had questions just like I did, and maybe you do as well. In John 3:3, Jesus tells Nicodemus, "Except a man be born again, he cannot see the kingdom of God." Nicodemus then asks the same question you are probably asking yourself right now, "How can a man be born when he is old?" Jesus says again in John 3:5, "Verily, verily, I say unto thee, except a man be born of water and of the Spirit, he cannot enter into the kingdom of God." Being born of the water is the physical birth. I think we can all agree we have been born, and yes, you must be born first before you can be born again, right? When I was born into the Harman family, I was born of water. This is the physical body, which will eventually die; but you see, Jesus came to save our souls, not our bodies. John 3:6 goes on to state, "That which is born of the flesh is flesh [physical]; and that which is born of the Spirit is spirit [your soul that lives forever]." Our bodies or flesh will be here on this earth and return to dust when we die, but our souls will live forever either in heaven or hell.

Since we are all sinners before a perfect and holy God, we are all facing eternal judgment in this place called hell; therefore, we need a spiritual birth, which we read about in John 1:12, "But as many as received him, to them gave he power to become the sons of God, even to them that believe on his name." I realized I was a sinner and on my way to hell, so I accepted Jesus Christ as my personal Savior. I was then born spiritually into the family of God. Anyone who will receive Jesus as Savior will be born again spiritually and placed into the family of God.

In Genesis 2, we read that God created one of the greatest institutions known to man: the family. The family is like a building, and just like any great building, it needs a solid foundation. In Genesis 2:18, God decided that man should not be alone. The passage continues,

> And the LORD God caused a deep sleep to fall upon Adam, and he slept (first anesthesiology): and he took one of his ribs, and closed up the flesh instead thereof (the first surgery); And the rib, which the LORD God had taken from man, made he a woman, and brought her unto the man. And Adam said, "This is now bone of my bones, and flesh of my flesh: she shall be called woman, because she was taken out of man. Therefore shall a man leave his father and his mother, and shall cleave unto his wife: and they shall be one flesh [the first marriage]." (Gen. 2:21–24)

This is the foundation of the family—man and woman—instituted by God, and I might add, long before the US Supreme Court. When a man joins in marriage with his wife, he is to commit himself wholeheartedly. They are two stones laid on the Rock, Jesus Christ, the ultimate foundation; and if the marriage is perverted or falls in any way, the family falls as well.

On October 21, 1989, I married my high school sweetheart, Rebecca. We stood before a church filled with friends and family and, of course, a preacher; but most importantly, we stood before God.

We made a commitment to love each other until death, no matter the circumstances. Even today I love her more than I did that cold day in October, and I thank the Lord for the happiness of these many years and counting. Of course, there have been difficulties, especially since I'm almost never wrong. But we made a commitment, and with the Lord's blessing, we will keep it for the rest of our lives. Jesus tells us in Matthew 19:6, "Wherefore they are no more twain (two) but one flesh, what therefore God hath joined together, let not man put asunder." The word *asunder* means to separate. God has joined man and woman as the foundation of the family, just like he joined my wife and me, and we are not to be separated. Marriage is a sacred picture of Christ and the church. "Husbands, love your wives, even as Christ also loved the church, and gave himself for it" (Eph. 5:25). Though man has failed in marriage, one thing is for sure, nothing can separate the church, those who are saved by the blood of Christ, from the love of God.

The family is to be built on the solid foundation of Jesus Christ. The church is built on that very same foundation. "And I say also unto thee, that thou art Peter, and upon this rock [Christ] I will build my church; and the gates of hell shall not prevail against it" (Matt. 16:18). Peter's name means stone or little rock. In other words, he is one of the stones in the foundation of the building, as were the other apostles.

> Now therefore ye are no more strangers and foreigners, but fellow-citizens with the saints, and of the household of God; And are built upon the foundation of the apostles and the prophets, Jesus Christ himself being the chief corner stone; In whom all the building fitly framed together groweth unto an holy temple in the Lord: In whom ye also are builded together for an habitation of God through the Spirit. (Eph. 2:19–22)

In those days, the building of a house or structure began by laying the chief cornerstone, a stone that was perfect in shape and size.

It was perfectly level, and all the other stones were then aligned from that stone for the foundation. The building was then fitly framed together, which meant each stone was purposefully and skillfully laid. The solid foundation of Jesus Christ is so strong that nothing can prevail against it or destroy it, not even Satan and his army. When we accept Jesus Christ as our Savior, we are children placed into the family of God and we are stones placed into the church, which sits on the foundation, Jesus Christ.

Jesus talks about two foundations in Matthew 7:24–27.

> Therefore whosoever heareth these sayings of mine, and doeth them, I will liken him unto a wise man, which built his house upon a rock: And the rain descended, and the floods came, and the winds blew, and beat upon that house; and it fell not: for it was founded upon a rock. And every one that heareth these sayings of mine, and doeth them not, shall be likened unto a foolish man, which built his house upon the sand: And the rain descended, and the floods came, and the winds blew, and beat upon that house; and it fell: and great was the fall of it.

What is your marriage or your family built upon? Or an even greater question, What is your faith built upon? Is it on that rock or sinking sand? Know that the storms will come and the winds will blow and beat you down. When a child is sick or a child rebels against you. Even greater, when a knock comes to your door and you receive word that a loved one has suddenly been taken from you by death, whether a child or a spouse. When you go to the doctor and you are diagnosed with cancer or some life-changing illness. These are storms, and they are strong and powerful. They can destroy a marriage, and they can topple a family. They can crush your faith and bring you to your knees, and oh, how great the fall of that building. But when we build on the Rock, the Lord Jesus Christ, that great, solid foundation, the storms may come but we will not be moved.

Growing up in the Harman family, my father and mother met our needs. I was the second of four children. We always had clothes on our backs and a warm place to stay, and we never went to bed hungry. Well, there were some exceptions, those nights when Mom made brown beans or fried liver for supper. How could anything smell so good and yet taste so bad? I just couldn't stand either one, so I would hide them in my napkin. And eventually, when that quit working, I would slip them under the seat cushion. That, of course, only worked until it began to ferment. If only we had a dog in the house! Then there were those times when, believe it or not, I just flat out got in trouble and had to go straight to bed without supper; nevertheless, our needs were always met.

Occasionally, we got things we really wanted but weren't necessarily considered needs. I can remember when I was around eight years old and I wanted a hunting dog so bad. I asked, but nothing ever really came of it, and time passed. Late one February evening, my grandfather pulled into the driveway with two purebred black-and-tan beagles, one for myself and one for my younger brother, Jason. Rascal and Freddie. My little brother, Jason, named every animal on the farm Fred; but since this was a female, we went with Freddie. By November, we were ready to go. With my little AH Fox 16-gauge double-barrel shotgun, we tore up the hillside. There wasn't a safe place in the area for a little cottontail rabbit. Mom fixed a lot of fried rabbit through those years. But looking back, I realize those beagles were still more of a want than a need, and it was a blessing to have them.

In the family of God, our Father supplies all of our needs and wants. All we have to do is come to Him and ask through prayer. "And all things, whatsoever ye shall ask in prayer, believing, ye shall receive" (Matt. 21:22). God provides for all His children. There is nothing too great or small. God cares for you. In fact, He knows you so well that He knows the number of hairs on your head. He knows your needs before you even ask. Since He loved you enough to die for you, don't you think He cares enough to meet your needs? Matthew 7:11 tells us, "If ye then, being evil, know how to give good gifts unto your children, how much more shall your Father which is in heaven give good things to them that ask him?" We are sinners, but our God is perfect. Be thankful that God knows your needs and your wants, and He will give you what is best if you ask and only believe.

God knows our needs and our desires, but He doesn't always give us what we want when we want it. This could be for several reasons. Many times we ask in unbelief. Jesus said, "If ye only believe." James 1:6–7 states, "But let him ask in faith, nothing wavering. For he that wavereth is like a wave of the sea driven with the wind and tossed. For let not that man think that he shall receive any thing of the Lord."

Sometimes we have sin in our lives. "But your iniquities have separated between you and your God, and your sins have hid his face from you, that he will not hear" (Isa. 59:2). Sin blocks fellowship. Have you ever asked your parents for something after getting caught in a lie? How did that go for you? Our God is no different. Confess that sin and get it right, and He will forgive you. There are times we ask amiss to consume things upon our own lusts. Rather than asking for something of which God would approve, we ask for things that would not be beneficial. Then there are times when we ask His will and our hearts are right, but He still doesn't seem to answer. Those are the times when He is teaching us patience and we need to keep praying and trusting. Sometimes He may answer right away, and those are the times we like the most, especially being in the age of instant gratification. But know that God always answers. It may be yes, it may be no, or it may be wait. But He always answers His children.

Being a parent requires great responsibility. There are many sleepless nights and prayerful days. It is our job as parents to nurture and admonish our children throughout their lives, not only through words but also by example. We are to influence our children, which can certainly be more effective.

Growing up in the Harman family, I was greatly influenced by my father. He taught me how to hunt and fish. I remember the warm spring and summer days when I was sitting on the riverbank and fishing for trout or smallmouth bass. I remember the crisp fall mornings when I was found under an old oak tree and was looking over a stand of hickories, watching a gray squirrel as he searched for his breakfast, and waiting for that perfect shot.

I was influenced by my grandfather as well. He hunted with hound dogs. Whether it was fox hunting or coon hunting, he loved to hear to those hounds chase. Every Friday night he would take the grandkids, usually three or four of us, and we would follow those hounds until late into the night. Many times in early fall, I have been awakened around one or two o'clock in the morning by the lonely sound of a hound chasing, and it brings back memories. I always prop my pillow up and sit and listen until they fade out into the night. All those nights we hunted, I don't think we ever killed the first raccoon, but we laughed until our sides were hurting. We learned a lot of things my mother or grandmother would deem inappropriate. He loved to tell jokes, and he was one of the best. No one else could tell them quite like he could, and I'm pretty sure he made them up as he went along. Of course, we also learned what would happen when we pulled his finger. That was always a crowd pleaser. Trust me, there are few things that make eight-year-old boys laugh, but that one never fails. Besides, how else are you going to keep four young boys entertained every Friday night? Yes, some things were inappropriate; but he taught us good life lessons as well, such as to look a man in the eye, shake his hand like you mean it, and don't give him a wet noodle!

When I was younger, he told me a story that stuck with me. My great-grandfather, Dr. Jabez Harman, was a medical doctor. He treated a man from the area we call Buffalo Mountain, which was several miles from town. The man had promised Dr. Jabez that he would come to his office to pay him on a certain day. It just happened on that day there was a blizzard, the worst storm of the year. Things were at a standstill, the area was paralyzed, and no one was going anywhere when they heard a knock at the door. It was the man from the Buffalo. He handed him the money he owed and said, "Thanks, Doc." He turned to walk away, and Dr. Jabez called out, "Sir, you didn't have to bring that in these conditions." The man replied, "I don't have many possessions or much money, but I do have my word, and without that, I have nothing." I have fallen short on that many times in my life, as we all have, but that is something I need to strive to do each day.

I am thankful for the influences in my life. My father and mother taught us about many things. We learned much about the Bible at church and at home. I remember having family devotions at home when I was a young boy. Mom would teach us the Bible, and I would teach her patience. Oh, how many times I would get the giggles, and she would pull out that switch. The harder she spanked me, the more I would laugh. As the proverb goes, "Train up a child in the way he should go and he will not depart from it." Mom and Dad did a lot of teaching, but thankfully, they spent a lot of time in prayer as well.

In the family of God, we are His children. We belong to Him. Just like a parent desires to see their children grow and become successful adults, God is no different. He desires to see us grow and to accomplish great things for His glory. "For we are his workmanship, created in Christ Jesus unto good works, which God hath before ordained that we should walk in them" (Eph. 2:10). When we trust Jesus Christ as our Savior, God takes a raw piece of clay and lays it on the potter's wheel to begin a new project. Through knowledge (the Word of God), through influence (the Holy Spirit), and through outside pressure (trials and tribulation), He will form that piece of clay into an object meet for the Master's use. I am a work in progress, no matter how perfect I may think I am. Rebecca reminds me of this fact on a regular basis. No, I am not perfect and won't be until I see my Savior face-to-face.

When we are born into the family of God, we are babes or babies in Christ, and it is God's desire that we grow. Peter tells us, "As newborn babes, desire the sincere milk of the word, that ye may grow thereby" (1 Pet. 2:2). God desires that each of us grow into a perfect or mature Christian man or woman. The baby's desire is for the mother's milk, and an infant must have milk to grow. When one accepts the gift of God and is born again, that child of God must also have a desire to be fed the sincere milk of the Word of God so that he or she might grow thereby.

Maddie was born in a litter of seven puppies. She didn't have any problems. She was always on top, and when it came to eating, she was the first one to the ninny. Of course, as is the case with many litters, there was one who was always rooted out. That poor little guy was always on the bottom and always last; he was the runt of the litter. He was the smallest, and he just let everyone else go first because he had no desire to eat. He didn't get the nourishment he needed to grow as he ought. Unfortunately, our churches are filled with runts, and I'm not referring to the physical sense. I guarantee you, have a church dinner and they will come out of the woodwork. No, rather than desiring the sincere milk of the Word, Christians today are desiring the things of the world. Entertainment and many other things manage to root their way into their lives, and they don't have the time or the desire for the Word of God. Therefore, they are runts, never growing to their potential.

A newborn baby needs milk to grow. Would you ever feed a newborn baby steak or corn on the cob? Of course not! The baby doesn't have the teeth to chew or the stomach to handle such food. A newborn Christian should desire to read the Bible and learn as much about our Lord as they can. Some desire to read the Bible through in a year. But many times they get into the book of Leviticus; become uninterested; and turn away, saying it's too hard, causing them to stumble and never grow in the Lord. I recommend that a newborn Christian begin reading in the book of John and then the other gospels to find out who Jesus is, learn the love of God, and why Jesus came to die for the sins of the world. This is the foundation of Bible-believing faith. Then study the Epistles and the Old Testament scriptures. This gives a basic understanding that everything from Genesis to Malachi and Matthew to Revelation revolves around Jesus Christ our Lord. Remember the Old Testament points to what Jesus Christ was going to do and the New Testament points back to what He has done, with the exception of the book of Revelation, which reveals what is to come. It helps also to find a good commentary for study, but keep in mind, a commentator is one person's view. Scripture has the final authority, not man. It's like someone once said, commentators are just common taters, so be careful.

Many times in studying, we will have difficulties understanding God's truths. That's when it helps to have a good mentor. I thank the Lord for my father, who has been a good mentor, as well as Clifton Brammer, who was my Sunday school teacher for many years. He not only mentored, but also encouraged me to do things I didn't think I could do. With him pushing and the Lord guiding, I found that just like Paul, "I can do all things through Jesus Christ which strengtheneth me." You will find, as I did, that if you are willing, God can use you in ways you never thought possible. As a Christian, if you have an opportunity to mentor someone, by all means don't neglect to do so. Mentoring is one of the greatest ministries you can have. Just be there for them, answer questions, lift them up, and encourage them. And if they ask something you cannot answer or do not know, don't be afraid to say, "I just don't know." I have studied the Bible for years, and there are things I still don't know and probably won't know until I get to heaven. Whatever you do, don't shoot from the hip. You don't want to lose the trust they have in you. Be honest, and take time to find the answer. If they need advice, be there to pray with them and seek the Lord's will in the matter. You are dealing with a young child in the Lord. Take it seriously. You may be leading the next great preacher.

Understanding the Bible can be difficult. It is good to have a good commentary and a good mentor, but nothing can take the place of the Author Himself. He freely gives the Holy Spirit to those who believe. Jesus promised when He left this world He would send "another comforter," which is the Holy Spirit, the third person of the Godhead. Don't ask me to explain the Godhead because I cannot comprehend it. Thankfully, God never commanded us to comprehend or even explain it but just by faith to believe it. Jesus says in John 14:26,

> But the Comforter, which is the Holy Ghost, whom the Father will send in my name, he shall teach you all things, and bring all things to your remembrance, whatsoever I have said unto you.

When we receive Jesus Christ as our Savior, God gives the Holy Spirit to indwell each believer. He will teach us all things. I am not by any means what you would call a well-educated man. Most of my studies have been on my own. I try to take a verse from the Bible and apply it to something I have dealt with, something in my surroundings or possibly to an event in history, even things going on in the world today. Honestly, there are times when my mind is blank, and I sit and stare at the same verse. But it's amazing how I can go to the Lord in prayer and ask Him to allow the Holy Spirit to teach me the things He has for me, and it's as if it jumps off the page. I can't help but wonder why I didn't see it before, but it's the Lord's work, just a simple answer to prayer.

Growing up in the Harman family, we had rules to keep. The rules included being respectful, especially to Mom and Dad; always using good manners; not fighting; and definitely not back talking. Yeah, try mumbling something under your breath, and see where it gets you. Sunday morning, Sunday night, and Wednesday night we were in church, no excuses. Growing up on a small forty-acre farm, we always had our daily chores, and the rule was that the chores had to be done.

In the family of God, we also have rules. We learn about these rules in the Bible. Jesus sums up the rules in just a few verses.

> Jesus said unto him, Thou shalt love the Lord thy God with all thy heart, and with all thy soul, and with all thy mind. This is the first and great commandment. And the second is like unto it, Thou shalt love thy neighbor as thyself. On these two commandments hang all the law and the prophets. (Matt. 22:37–40)

This is God's perfect law in a nutshell, how we treat God and how we treat our fellow man. In order to be in His presence, we must keep God's perfect standard. Now some people believe we can and must keep that standard, and by doing so, they become a member of the family of God. There are those who believe we must accept Jesus

Christ as our Savior to become a member of God's family, but that we must keep that standard in order to remain in the family of God, meaning that if we sin, we somehow disqualify ourselves and lose our salvation or that God would disown us as His children. Others believe that salvation is totally through Jesus Christ and His finished work alone and that we can receive the gift through believing and accepting Him as our personal Savior.

Let's look first at the commandment. Jesus said to love the Lord your God with all your heart, mind, and soul. Can you honestly say you love the Lord in that capacity, with your entire being, everything you have? This love is the same sacrificial love in which He loved you and me. It is a love that produces obedience and sacrifice to Him. We see how this command compares to the first of the Ten Commandments: "Thou shalt have no other Gods before me." Anything we put before God becomes an idol, a god that we are not to put before Him. Think about our jobs, hobbies, entertainment, and other things. If we love Him to the capacity He would have us to love Him, we would sacrifice all these things to love Him, but we don't, and we therefore have broken that commandment. It was impossible for us to keep it in the first place.

Let's try the other command. Maybe we can be successful there. "Thou shalt love thy neighbor as thyself." It is the same self-sacrificial love to which Jesus was referring when He said to "love one another as I have loved you." The question we ask is, Who is thy neighbor? Thy neighbor is anyone with whom we come in contact. It could be your friend or your worst enemy. In the Ten Commandments, we are told to not steal, commit adultery, or kill. We think these things don't seem too hard to keep, but Jesus said that if we so much as think or desire to do one of them, we have already committed that sin in our hearts. I have heard married men make the comment, "Just because you are on a diet doesn't mean you can't look at the menu." But that look is sin in the eyes of God. Then there is the commandment about bearing false witness, or lying. The little white lies, the half-truths—they are all lies. They are all sin. Thou shalt not covet, or desire, something that isn't yours. This is a tough one, especially in the age of media. We are bombarded by commercials on television and enticed continually, keeping us always wanting and never satisfied. With one bad thought or action, we can easily break the law. If we love our neighbors the way Jesus says to love, we would not commit these sins toward our neighbors, but in our failures, we prove once again that it is impossible to do. We are all sinners before a perfect and Holy God.

Peter disputed with those who taught that the Law must be kept for salvation and asked this question: "Now therefore why tempt ye God, to put a yoke upon the neck of the disciples, which neither our fathers nor we were able to bear?" (Acts 15:10). Back in those days, a yoke was used on the oxen to hook up the load for the oxen to pull. Growing up, we used a harness to pull the load with a work horse. Of course, it's a lot easier now; it's called a hitch on a Chevrolet truck or a John Deere tractor, but the same principle. Jesus tells the disciples in Matthew 11:28–30,

> Come unto me, all ye that labor and are heavy laden, and I will give you rest. Take my yoke upon you, and learn of me; for I am meek and lowly in heart: and ye shall find rest for your souls. For my yoke is easy, and my burden is light.

Peter says the yoke was too heavy and no one is able to bear it. Jesus says to lay down that yoke and take His yoke, which is light, because He has already done the work for salvation. Put your faith and trust in Him, accept the gift of the work on the cross, and He will give you rest. Peter goes on to say in Acts 15:11, "But we believe that through the grace of the LORD Jesus Christ we shall be saved, even as they."

Years ago, I was teaching a teen class on this very subject. I went to the dry-erase board and made two sets of points, *A* and *B*. I asked two students to draw a straight line in freehand to the best of their ability from point *A* to *B*. Both lines seemed to be pretty straight, but then I took a straight edge and drew a line parallel between the two lines they had drawn. When comparing the lines to the perfectly straight line, we discovered they weren't as straight as we thought.

In our lives, we may think that we are doing pretty good; but when we compare our lives to the Law, God's perfect standard, we realize we are not even close. In fact, it is impossible for us to be perfect. The Law is our school master and teaches us just how sinful we are before a righteous and perfect God. Why carry the yoke you cannot bear? When we accept Jesus, we take on His perfect righteousness and carry His light yoke, giving each of us rest for our souls.

There are those who believe we are saved by faith in Jesus Christ; but at some time in their lives, they can commit sin, causing them to lose their salvation. Therefore, that one must continually be saved. God instituted the family because he knew it was the best way to raise children, but it is also a picture of his future family, the church. The Old Testament is full of pictures and types, examples that you and I may learn. One example is the children of Israel wandering in the wilderness. You can study this story in Exodus 17. To paraphrase, the children of Israel had come out of Egypt, and there was no fresh water, so they complained to Moses they would die if they didn't have fresh water. God told Moses that along the way there would be a rock in Horeb. Moses was to take his staff and smite, or strike, the rock; and as soon as he struck the rock, fresh water would come pouring out for the people to drink. This is a picture of Jesus Christ. As the Rock, He was smitten for our sins, and He died on the cross. Through his death, we have the Holy Spirit, gushing out freely for all who believe and receive that gift. Our thirst will then be quenched. Fast-forward to Numbers 20:8 when the children of Israel were having a similar crisis and they needed fresh water. God told Moses to speak to the rock this time and water would come out. Why would God tell Moses to speak rather than strike it as He did before? Because it is a picture of the crucifixion of Jesus Christ, the Rock, who can only be smitten and die once. Jesus Christ was crucified for our sins. He was that perfect sacrifice, and He paid the price in full as He cried, "It is finished!" He cannot be crucified again. Once we accept Jesus Christ as our Savior, we can come to Him in prayer and speak to Him. It is through prayer we have our needs met and sins forgiven. If He has already saved us, why then do we continue to crucify Him every time we sin? He paid it *all!* Jesus said that ye must be born again, not again, again, and again. If salvation can be lost, then we have to keep going back, and we end up striking the rock continually when all we have to do is speak to Him. Out of frustration, Moses struck the rock the second time rather than speaking to it, and in doing so, he destroyed the picture and lost his reward.

Let's compare the natural family with the family of God. I was born physically of my father and my mother. There is nothing I can do that will change that fact. You can check my DNA. There is no way around it. Now I am ashamed to say this, but as I got older, my father and I had some heated rounds and said things that were offensive to him, things I now regret. I'm sure in those times and probably many others, he would like to disown me, but no matter the circumstance, I am still his son. That is impossible to change.

One year my daughter gave me a coffee cup for Father's Day. It had the inscription, "I smile because you are my dad. I laugh because there is nothing you can do about it." Oh, so true. When we are born again, we are born into the family of God, and we cannot be disowned or removed. Jesus tells us in John 10:27–29,

> My sheep hear my voice, and I know them, and they follow me: And I give unto them eternal life; and they shall never perish, neither shall any man pluck them out of my hand. My Father, which gave them me, is greater than all; and no man is able to pluck them out of my Father's hand.

Are you greater than God that you can pluck yourself out of God's hand? Is your sin or Satan himself so great that they can separate you from your Father in heaven?

> For I am persuaded, that neither death, nor life, nor angels, nor principalities, nor powers, nor things present, nor things to come, nor height, nor depth, nor any other creature, shall be able to separate us from the love of God, which is in Christ Jesus our Lord. (Rom. 8:38–39)

Nothing can separate us from our Savior as Hebrews tells us, "He is able to save us to the uttermost." In Ephesians 2:20–22, we are told that we are a building fitly framed together. If you were building a stone wall and you decided that the stones halfway up the wall didn't suit you so began pulling them out, what kind of wall would you have? It would be like a game of Jenga; the wall would become weak and fall. The church is God's building. We who believe are born again and are placed into that building, and it is so strong the gates of hell shall not prevail against it. Ephesians 4:16 refers to the church as the body of Christ. We are the members, or body parts, as He is the head. Imagine if the members are removed because they are not suitable any longer. Wouldn't that make the body of Christ handicapped? Christ and His body are perfect, without blemish because of His perfect righteousness. Either you have eternal life or you don't. There is no in-between. When we are saved, we are saved to the uttermost for all eternity. "For whosoever believeth in him shall have eternal life."

Now that brings us to the question everyone wants to ask: If you cannot lose your salvation, then that gives you a license to sin and do whatever you want, right? Wrong! Let's go back to the physical family. I remember many times as a kid I would leave the gate open or forget to latch the gate; and then one or more of the animals, usually more, would get out into the road, or worse yet, into the garden. Of course, I would always confess, "It wasn't me." And yes, with three kids of my own, I'm getting paid back now. But needless to say, the truth would eventually come out. I would have to pay for that sin, most of the time with a blistering hickory switch on my backside, more for lying than for leaving the gate open; but I learned really quickly not to leave it open again, at least for a few days anyway. In the family of God, there are times we will sin and our Father in heaven will need to chasten us, which by definition means to "child train." In Hebrews 12:6, we read, "For whom the Lord loveth He chasteneth, and scourgeth every son whom he receiveth." We are the Lord's children, and He wants each of us to grow into mature Christians for His glory. Therefore, He must train us through chastening. He also allows trials to come into our lives. The trials strengthen us and prepare us to be

His servants. When your child disobeys you, do you have him executed? Of course not! So why, after He has promised us eternal life, would our loving Father in heaven send us to hell when we are disobedient? This makes no sense, especially since God is long-suffering and not willing that any should perish. We all hate to be punished, but it is comforting to know God only trains His children, those who believe. "But if ye be without chastisement, whereof all are partakers, then ye are bastards, and not sons" (Heb. 12:8).

Being a family member requires each child to have responsibility. Right in the middle of the Ten Commandments is the command that sums up all the commands for the child: "Honour thy father and thy mother: that thy days may be long upon the land which the LORD thy God giveth thee" (Exod. 20:12). The word *honor* means to love, revere, or respect to the point of obedience. This commandment puts the parents in authority over their children as God instituted, not the children over the parents as seems to be the case today. God put the parents over the children as they grow so they could nurture and teach the children the things of God. Unfortunately, we live in a time where children are not taught the things of God; therefore, children do not respect their parents and have become disobedient. To go a step further, the lack of respect and disobedience in the home carries over into our school system and in society in general. Over time, we will have a generation that does not know God. We are seeing this now in the United States the fruits of the lack of teaching in the home, a godless society and a lawless people. When the family falls, the nation comes crashing down on top of it. God loves His children and punishes us when we disobey Him; therefore, we need to obey Him.

I want to bring to your attention to one more statement that Jesus made in John 14:15. "If you love me, keep my commandments." The first of the two great commandments is "Love the Lord thy God with all your heart, mind and soul." When you were born into your family, did you love your parents? No, all you were concerned about was yourself, eating and sleeping and making sure everyone knew when you had a dirty diaper. When you trusted Jesus Christ as your Savior, did you trust Him because you loved Him? No, you trusted Him because you didn't want to go to hell but rather to heaven. You did it for your own benefit. As you got older, did you obey your parents because you loved them or was it because you were afraid you would be punished? I know I obeyed because if I didn't, I would get a good tail busting. As Christians grow, they learn about the things of God and try to obey out of a reverential respect for the Lord, but many times they obey out of fear of punishment. As we grow into teenagers and young adults—and trust me, it takes some longer than others—we begin to do things out of the love of our heart for our parents. We have formed a relationship. Our obedience is no longer for personal gain or out of fear but out of love. As Christians mature, they develop a relationship with the Lord, and they obey the Lord out of a heart of love. Since Jesus told us to "love one another as I have loved you," that self-sacrificial agape love, doesn't it stand to reason we should love Him as He loved us? Agape love is not an emotional love; it is a love of action and obedience.

With this in mind, let's think again to the first commandment: "Thou shalt have no other gods before me." The Christian who has developed a loving relationship with the Lord says, "I love you, Lord. I don't want any other gods before you." All through the commandments, when God says, "Thou shalt not," the mature Christian once again says, "I don't want to, Lord, I love you. The Lord is the center of my life. My will is His will. My desire is His desire, and I obey His commandments because I want to please Him. Sure, I can sin and not lose my salvation and my Father in heaven could chastise me for that sin, but that doesn't matter because I want to bring glory to my God in my life." Paul tells us in 1 Corinthians 10:31, "Whether therefore ye eat, or drink, or whatsoever ye do, do all to the glory of God." If you are trying to earn your way into heaven, you are seeking your own salvation for your own benefit; and if you could possibly be successful, which is proven impossible, you would receive the glory. Paul tells us again in Ephesians 2:8–9, "For by grace are ye saved through faith: and that not of yourselves: it is the gift of God: Not of works, lest any man should boast." There will be no boasting in heaven of what we have accomplished. All the glory will go to Jesus Christ our Lord for His finished work on the cross. Salvation is by grace through faith, so leave it at the cross. Satan will do everything he can to cause you to doubt the Lord and trust in your own works, but trust the Lord and do all to glorify Him.

Though we strive for perfection to live a sinless life, we want so much to be obedient to God whom we love, but we continually fall short of His glory. I remember as a young boy, I really wanted to be a good boy. Unfortunately, good and boy don't always go together unless maybe you put tired or sleeping in there somewhere. I would always seem to get in trouble, and my father would look at me like he could kill me, and there were times I thought he would. After it was all over, I could go to him, confess, and apologize for what I had done. And even though I had suffered the consequences, he would always forgive me, and we would put it behind us. We can be thankful that our Father in heaven also forgives us. "If we confess our sins, he is faithful and just to forgive us our sins, and to cleanse us from all unrighteousness" (1 John 1:9). If we sin—and we will because we are not perfect—all we have to do is go to our Heavenly Father and confess our sins to Him, and He will cleanse us from that sin. The psalmist writes in Psalm 103:12, "As far as the east is from the west, so far hath he removed our transgressions from us." Thank God, He doesn't remove the child, but instead, He forgives and removes the sin. If God removed a child each time we sinned, there wouldn't be anyone in heaven, and it would be a sad place.

God the Father cares and desires the best for His children. He cares enough to discipline and to teach in order that we may be perfect, or mature, Christians, vessels used for His glory. He cares enough to allow us to be a part of His work in evangelizing, telling others about Christ, so that they also may be saved and enter into the family of God. He cares enough to give us the ability to teach and disciple young Christians so they may grow in the Lord. God is good to His children, and in His love, He desires that all come to repentance and be in His family. That's why He sent His son to the cross to die for the whole world, that whosoever believeth in Him would be saved.

Are you in the family of God? If not, trust Him today. Maybe you have doubts about your salvation and you have lived in fear not knowing if some sin you committed has cost you eternal life. Maybe you think God is done with you, that because of something in your life, there is no possible way He could forgive you. Understand that the Lord is compassionate and of tender mercy. As Jesus hung on that cross, He cried, "It is finished." The price was paid in full. God accepted that sacrifice as He raised Him from the grave on the third day. He had the power to pay for all of the sins of the world, and there is no sin too great for Him to forgive.

The Lord desires that you come to Him. He wants to forgive you. He wants you to be His child. He wants a relationship with you today, but you have to come to Him. Finally, live a Christ-centered life, and desire to serve Him in everything you do. Strive to be obedient to His will for your life and seek that fellowship as a father and his child so you can say, as John would, "That your joy may be full." What joy we have in the family of God!

THE HEART OF A BIRD DOG

Bilbo's Maddie Moo, aka Maddie, is a Brittany spaniel. Standing around twenty-two inches tall and weighing about thirty-five pounds, she is a bundle of pent-up energy. Maddie is white with large brown patches over her body. Her head is brown with a white blaze running down her face, and like most Brittanys, she has freckles all over her nose. While her little ears are brown and wiry, she has a bobbed tail that she wags constantly especially when she is hunting.

Hunting is Maddie's greatest desire, and that is when she is happiest. Maddie always has a happy expression; she always seems to be smiling. With such an expression, I find it difficult to fuss at her, no matter what she does. Needless to say, Maddie is spoiled rotten. Her kennel has two large fireplaces, and she curls up in front of them to stay warm the winter. She also has two heat pumps to keep her cool in the summer. I feel privileged that she allows us to live with her in her elaborate kennel. While Rebecca furthers her medical education, she studies many hours in our bed. Maddie is always right by her side. Maddie also enjoys watching the Food Network as well as Fox News on occasion but gets bored with that pretty easily. Her favorite show was *Wingshooting USA* on the Sportsman Channel. She would get excited when she heard the whistles blow or the thunderous sound of the pheasant's wings as it propelled itself upward like a helicopter out of the tall grass. Maddie sleeps downstairs at night; but in the morning, she will come busting through the door of our bedroom, only to root her way under the covers between Rebecca and me, forcing us to get out of bed. Rebecca has told me more than once, "You love that dog more than you love me." That remark reminds me of a story I once heard about my grandfather.

My grandfather was a man who loved his dogs. In his younger days, he kept several foxhounds. At the time, he was dating a beautiful girl who also happened to be the daughter of the judge. Evidently, they were in a pretty serious relationship at the time. Sunday was a special day, probably a church social or homecoming, and all the women were dressed in their best dresses. The women had spent hours preparing themselves as well as baking food over the last few days, each one wanting to outdo the others as they brought out their best. After the church service, everyone went outside to the picnic area. This was a big event in such a small town. Everyone would attend, even my grandfather who never darkened the door of any church. The morning had come and gone, the service was over, and there was no sign of my grandfather anywhere. As prayer was being offered and lunch was served, everyone heard in the distance an old 1929 Ford pickup truck clucking down the road accompanied by the sound of howling dogs riding on the back of the truck and followed by a cloud of dust. My grandfather had been out fox hunting all night and was just getting back as he had done so many times before. He pulled up into the church parking lot with a grin on his face. I'm sure proud of himself for a successful hunt and, of course, just the fact that he made it to the event. But let me tell you, he got a chewing like he had never gotten before. With her hands on her hips and her face red with embarrassment and anger, the judge's daughter gritted her teeth and yelled at the top of her lungs, "Chris Harman, you are going to have to make a choice. It's either me or those stinkin' dogs!" He thought just a second, and with a grin on his face, he replied, "I think a lot of my damn dogs." He drove off never looking back. Yeah, I think a lot of my dog; but, Rebecca, you're still number one.

Maddie likes to lie in bed and eat suckers, and the way she sprawls out on her back with her feet up in the air, you would think that girl was worthless, but when the door opens on the truck and we hit the woods, she is all business. Today is no different. She seems to have picked up the scent of a grouse. Her tail is wagging a little faster, and her nose is to the ground. She swings over into a thicket. It is full of green briars and crab apple trees with long thorns. Several of the branches have fallen from past years and made it difficult to penetrate, but they don't seem to slow her down. As she crawls on her belly and nudges her way deep into the thicket, I can barely see her. She moves a little farther, and I manage to see the tip of her tail, now stained with blood. She appears to be stuck but then alters her direction slightly and pushes through it. She is so focused on her job and the task at hand that nothing else matters. She moves a little farther and stops on a dime. With her tail up and her nose down, she freezes like a statue. She is on a point. Maddie is a bird dog; her purpose is to hunt birds. Also man's best friend, she is devoted to pleasing her master. No matter how tough it gets, she is focused on doing those things. This is the heart of a bird dog.

What if we were willing to serve our Master, the Lord Jesus Christ, to that capacity? A good bird dog loves its master and will always be loyal. Do you love the Lord? Will you be loyal to Him? Just like Maddie, we have a Master to serve. The road will be rough and sometimes seem impossible. Like Maddie, we will feel pain and sorrow. In fact, many times we will suffer in our work; but in all of our pain and suffering, by our faith and in love, we will point, not to a bird, but to our Lord Jesus Christ, the one who loved us, suffered for us, and bought us with the price of His precious blood.

Several years ago I decided to get into bird hunting. I had hunted with my father since I was a young boy, so I had a little experience. One thing I needed was a good bird dog. I looked around at several puppies, but never really found one I wanted. Finally, I heard about a gentleman who owned a one-year-old Brittany spaniel. He was no longer able to hunt and therefore couldn't put in the training required to make her the dog she should be, so he gave her to me. I had a little experience hunting but not the knowledge to train a dog. Little did I know she would end up being the teacher. Yes, she taught me how to hunt. They say you will only have one great bird dog in a lifetime. I was fortunate enough to start with one. I bred her to Maddie's great-grandfather, Bilbo, and kept the best female, Sophie. One Thanksgiving, we were hunting along a river bottom. Sophie was only a year old at the time and didn't have much experience. We worked along the bottom, and the dogs pointed. As we walked in, the grouse flushed. I shot and dropped it right in the middle of the river. I thought, *Now how am I going to get that bird?* The water was freezing cold. Before I could say anything, Sophie ran and dived right into the river, swam out to the middle, grabbed the bird, and laid it at my feet. I couldn't believe it, but I acted as if she did things like that all the time. Of course, it also gave me a chance to brag a little to my hunting partners. You know everything is a competition, and I had to rub it in that my dog was the best.

So what makes a bird dog special? What makes them desire to point and to fulfill the purpose that you have for them? It's all in the breeding. It's in their nature. It comes from the heart. It comes from within. How can we serve the Lord the way He would have us to serve? Before we can truly serve the Lord, we must have a heart that is ready and willing. It must be our desire from within and not just an outward motion. In order to have that heart, we must first be born again. I cannot emphasize that enough. Paul tells us in 2 Corinthians 5:17, "Therefore if any man be in Christ (born again), He is a new creature: old things are passed away; behold, all things are become new." When we receive Jesus Christ as our Savior, we receive a new nature, a new heart. Before salvation, I could not serve the Lord because my desire was for myself. My old nature is selfishness. My new nature is servanthood, a desire to serve Him as my Master. We must understand one thing. Even though we have a new nature, the old nature hasn't disappeared. It is still there. In fact, it is going to be at war with the new nature until we leave this earth.

> For the flesh (the old sinful nature) lusteth against (desires against or is in opposition to) the Spirit, (the Holy Spirit and the new nature) and the Spirit against the flesh: and these things are contrary the one to the other: so that ye cannot do the thing that ye would. (Gal. 5:17)

Sometimes it seems so difficult to do the right thing. We so often fall short and sin against God, but we are not alone. The apostle Paul struggled with these things just like we do today. "For the good that I would I do not: but the evil which I would not, that I do" (Rom. 7:19). Does that sound like your life? It sure sounds like mine. I have to be the first to admit that I have allowed that old nature to win. So many times, just like Paul, I knew what was right, I wanted to do right, but I didn't. I should have taken a stand. I should have told that one about Christ. Then there are the evil thoughts that I allowed into my mind, the things I said or things I have done that I shouldn't have. I could go on and on. Unfortunately, I knew what was wrong, and yet I did it anyway.

Maddie has been trained to heel, and she knows when I make that command. But sometimes she gets so excited, breaks, and runs ahead. She knows what to do, but her natural instinct tells her to go. She also knows when she points, it is her job to hold until I flush the bird. If she doesn't, the bird takes off before I get a shot, defeating the purpose of the point. When I see her point, I tell her to whoa, meaning she is not to move until I release with the command to break. Even though her purpose is to point and the command is to hold, her selfish nature is to break and catch the bird for herself. Sounds like Paul, sounds like me, and, probably if you will be honest with yourself, sounds like you. We are born with a sinful nature, making it natural for us to sin and serve ourselves, but when we are saved, that new nature confronts the old sinful nature. Sometimes the old nature wins; and many times we give it that victory by allowing it to control our lives, defeating the purpose our Lord has for us and causing us to lose our ability to serve the Lord with the heart He desires.

The old nature is very powerful. We need help to defeat that nature, and we cannot do it on our own. God gave us the tools to help in this battle with the flesh. God, being all-wise and knowing, gave us His Word, the Bible, and also the privilege of prayer. His Word leads us on the right path, and through prayer, we can ask for wisdom to live the way He would have us to live. It's like He gives us a map, and we can call Him and ask for directions any time we get turned around. The problem we have is that many times we don't know what to pray for nor can we understand the Word of God. Therefore, we are ignorant of His direction. Thankfully, our God understands all of our shortcomings and that we need help. That is why Jesus made a promise to send help before He went to the cross to die for our sins. "And I will pray the Father, and he shall give you another Comforter, that he may abide with you forever" (John 14:16). "Comforter" refers to one called alongside to help. John goes on to say, "But the Comforter, which is the Holy Ghost, whom the Father will send in my name, he shall teach you all things, and bring all things to your remembrance, whatsoever I have said unto you" (John 14:26). The one "called alongside to help" is the Holy Ghost, or the Holy Spirit. The Holy Spirit teaches us the things we need to know and truths in the Bible because we cannot understand them on our own. He brings truths we have studied to our attention when we so desperately need those words to guide our lives, direct our paths, and defeat that old nature. Now we can have a road map and one to help us understand the directions. The Holy Spirit helps us to become the servants God would have us to become so that we might live victoriously over sin and Satan.

The Holy Spirit gives us knowledge, helps us remember, and convicts our hearts. The Holy Spirit gives us a thirst and a desire to quench that thirst. Have you ever been so thirsty and couldn't find anything to quench your thirst? Maybe you have a thirst in your life. Nothing seems to satisfy. You have gotten that job you always wanted; have accumulated wealth, a car and a house; and found a relationship with that special one in your life. But there is still something missing. You are seeking things that cannot satisfy, and the Holy Spirit is dealing with you. Jesus says in John 6:35, "He that believeth on me shall never thirst."

Only Jesus can quench that thirst and save you from your sins. Only through Jesus can we drink at the springs of living water. As Christians, we serve our God, and the battle rages on. Many times we don't realize it, but the sin nature is controlling our lives. That is when the Holy Spirit convicts our hearts. The Holy Spirit is that fire that burns within us when we sin against our Lord, the fire that fuels that guilty feeling and eats at us until we confess that sin before God and make it right in our lives, but we must listen to the Spirit. It is dangerous for anyone, whether in salvation or service, to ignore the Holy Spirit tugging at your heartstrings. First Thessalonians 5:19 tells us, "Quench not the Spirit." When the Spirit convicts us, we have a choice. We can repent or continue in that sin. The word *quench* means simply to put out. First Timothy 4:2 states, "Speaking lies in hypocrisy; having their conscience seared with a hot iron."

Quench and *seared*, though different analogies, have the same principle meaning. If a fire is burning, we quench that fire by dowsing it with water. We likewise can quench the Spirit by covering up our sins as if they never happened, in turn lying to ourselves and continuing in that sin until it no longer hurts. Many times, one who is running from the Lord will ignore the thirst that the Holy Spirit gives until he or she is no longer concerned. The Lord wants so much for you to be saved. He is calling you, He is pricking your heart, and He is giving you that thirst. Unfortunately, there will come a time when it is too late. They will continue to ignore the Spirit, filling their lives with pleasures, until they have become so callused that they have quenched the Holy Spirit. Don't dowse the fire. Don't ignore the pain. Turn to Him before it is everlasting too late.

This time of year the leaves begin to fall from the trees and clutter our yards. We grab our rakes and head out for a long day's work. We must keep our yards immaculate, making sure our yard looks better than the neighbor down the street. After hours of constant raking, you look down and see your hand has become red with a painful blister. Your body is telling you to stop and put on a pair of gloves to prevent further damage, and yet you ignore the pain and keep on going. It heals up over the next few days, and more leaves begin to fall, so you grab your rake and go after it once again. You then look down at your hands and realize they don't hurt any longer. Your hands have become hard and callused, and you can no longer feel the pain. When we are convicted of sin and the fire of guilt burns within our hearts but we continue on, ignoring the pain, soon our hearts become callused to the Holy Spirit's moving until we have quenched the Spirit. As Christians, we can become callused and quench the Spirit, and when we have quenched him, we can no longer serve in the way God would have us to serve. In fact, our hearts can turn from service to selfishness until we repent and make things right. Want to be a servant of Christ? Want to serve him with the heart of a bird dog? Listen! Quench not the Spirit!

The greatest example we have of a servant is none other than Jesus Christ Himself. Yes, our Lord Jesus Christ came to die for our sins. He was a servant even unto death; but before His death, burial, and resurrection, He taught his disciples. One thing He taught was servanthood, and our Lord never taught anything He didn't do Himself. Everything he taught was not only by word but also by example. Paul writes in the book of Philippians 2:5–8,

> Let this mind be in you, which is also in Christ Jesus: Who, being in the form of God, thought it not robbery to be equal with God: But made himself of no reputation, and took upon him the form of a servant, and was made in the likeness of men: And being found in fashion as man, he humbled himself, and became obedient unto death, even the death of the cross.

Even though Jesus was God in the flesh, He came as a servant. Jesus had a purpose; and He focused completely on that purpose, to seek and to save that which was lost, to make a way for man to come to God. Why did Christ leave heaven's glory to die on a cross? How could one so great become a servant? Love and humility! He loved us enough to give His life, and He humbled Himself enough to hang on a cross so that the perfect sacrifice for sin would be made. "For scarcely for a righteous man will one die; yet peradventure for a good man some would even dare die; But God commended his love toward us, in that, while we were yet sinners, Christ died for us" (Rom. 5:7–8). Christ our Lord loved us so much that He came as a servant to die for his enemies, you and me.

Our Lord showed His love throughout His earthly ministry. He hated to see men suffer. So out of a heart of compassion, one by one, He healed them, proving Himself the great physician. He went place to place teaching man the love of God and warning them of the coming judgment and the lake of fire if they didn't repent and accept Him as Savior. He pleaded with them, "Come unto me and I will give you rest. …Come unto me and you will never hunger or thirst." Our Lord is not willing that any should perish, but that all should come to repentance. In love and humility, He was never concerned about His well-being. He knew the plan, and He knew the purpose.

As foxes have holes and birds have nests, our Lord didn't have a place to lay his head. The God of creation should have been born in the most elaborate palace known to man; but in humility, He was born in a stall, wrapped in grave clothes, and laid in a feed trough. As He entered into his friend's house, the trumpets should have sounded; and everyone should have fallen down before Him in worship, crying out, "The great Messiah!" But in humility, as a servant, He washed the feet of the disciples. He should have been proclaimed King of kings! But in love and humility, He was beaten beyond recognition, mocked, and laughed to scorn. They spit in his face and ultimately hung him on a cross and said, "We'll not have this man to rule over us." He hung on that cross naked yet clothed in shame. He could have called ten thousand angels to save Him and destroy the world, but in love for all mankind, He humbled himself, and in obedience, He died between two thieves. Do you ever feel like no one loves you? Do you feel like no one cares? The God of creation loves you. Look what He has done for you.

As a Christian, maybe you don't know how to serve. Learn from the example of the very one that saved you. As a servant, on the night of his arrest, Jesus went to the Father in prayer. "Father, if thou be willing, remove this cup from me: nevertheless not my will, but thine, be done" (Luke 22:42). Jesus was more concerned with accomplishing the Father's will than He was about His own life. He was more concerned about you and me and paying for the sins of the world than anything else He could possibly gain. Our Lord had a heart of a servant, far greater than the heart of any bird dog. Jesus says in Mark 9:35, "If any man desire to be first, the same shall be last of all, and servant of all." Many people want to be leaders, but in order to lead, we must first learn to serve.

One of the greatest missionaries to ever live was Paul. Like all of us, Paul was a sinful man. He was a self-righteous Pharisee, one of the religious elite. He was a zealous man and dedicated his life to religion and destroying the name of Jesus Christ and the church. It was Paul standing by at the stoning of Stephen. It was Paul who took orders to go to Damascus and arrest Christians, but it was Jesus Christ who met him on the way and changed his life forever. When Jesus brings you to your knees, you will never be the same. When Paul turned to Jesus, the Lord took his zeal and used it for His glory. Paul began at least fourteen churches between Jerusalem and Rome; he wrote thirteen books of the New Testament; and he was beaten, stoned, left for dead and thrown in prison. Yet he still carried the good news of the gospel all the way to Rome. If that wasn't enough, Paul was eventually beheaded for the cause of Christ. On the road to Damascus, he traded his pride for humility and his hatred for the church into a love for sinners. He writes in 1 Corinthians 13, "Without charity (sacrificial love) I am nothing." Paul lived a Christ-centered life. He was a servant to the core. He gave his life to Christ on that road to Damascus, and he never took it back. Paul had a servant's heart. He had the heart of a bird dog. How about you? Did you give your heart to Christ? Did you try to take it back? Are you truly serving the Lord today?

What does it mean to serve the Lord Jesus Christ? When we think of servants of God, we think of pastors or missionaries, maybe a Sunday school teacher or musician. These are great ways to serve, but not everyone is called to fill these positions. So do you just not serve? Of course not. There are many ways we can serve without being in full-time ministry. I am reminded of 1 Corinthians 10:31: "Whether therefore ye eat, or drink, or whatsoever ye do, do all to the glory of God." This verse tells us that even down to the simplest things that we do in life, we can glorify God. And when we are glorifying, we are worshipping, and when we are worshipping, we are serving. Just by a simple prayer before you eat gives thanksgiving and praise for what He has given. David says in Psalm 100:2–4,

> Serve the Lord with gladness: come before
> his presence with singing. Know ye that the Lord
> he is God: it is he that hath made us, and not we
> ourselves; we are his people, and the sheep of his
> pasture. Enter into his gates with thanksgiving,
> and into his courts with praise: be thankful unto
> him, and bless his name.

Worship with thanksgiving and praise, for without Him, we are nothing.

God designed us to worship. From creation, He programmed each of us to be in awe. We can see this as we watch great athletes who perform seemingly miraculous plays and musicians who mesmerize us with their music and great talent. This is worship. I grew up watching Walter Payton juke and break tackles. It seemed no one could bring him down or stop him when he would dive over the pile into the end zone to score a touchdown. Then there was Michael Jordan, who would fly over the defender to slam dunk the basketball. He made moves that seemed impossible, and we watched in amazement. These acts drew praise from the spectators. This is worship. The musicians with talent and skill are worshipped and idolized by our young people today. We are programmed to worship, and we will worship something or someone. But there is only one that is truly worthy of worship, the very one that saved us from our sins: our Lord and Savior Jesus Christ. The great athletes and musicians will pass on and will be forgotten, and someone else will come on the scene and take their place. The name of Jesus will go on for eternity.

> Wherefore God also hath highly exalted him, and given him a name which is above every name: That at the name of Jesus every knee should bow, of things in heaven, and things in earth, and things under the earth; And that every tongue should confess that Jesus Christ is Lord, to the glory of God the Father. (Phil. 2:9–11)

Want to serve the Lord with a servant's heart? Only He is worthy of praise and honor, and He will one day receive that praise from all creation, when every knee bows to Him. He is the Creator of the universe. He loved us so much that He lived a sinless life, hung on a cross, died, and was buried. And yet He had the power to rise again on the third day, declaring those who put their faith in Him righteous so that we might have a relationship with Him and one day spend eternity in His very presence. Only He is worthy to be praised!

Either you can acknowledge that He is Lord here on earth or you can acknowledge Him at the great white throne judgment and be cast into the lake of fire forever and ever, but either way every knee will bow to Him and every tongue will confess that Jesus is Lord.

We serve God through worship, but we also serve God through obedience. In order to be a true servant of the Lord, obedience is a priority. Jesus said, "If you love me, keep my commandments." This is serving God with a heart of love. We keep His commandments because we love Him. Before we can serve the Lord in any part of our lives, we must obey His very first command to believe. "For God so loved the world, that he gave his only begotten Son, that whosoever believeth in him should not perish, but have everlasting life" (John 3:16). Paul and Silas tell the prison keeper in Acts 16:31, "Believe on the Lord Jesus Christ, and thou shalt be saved, and thy house." It is impossible to serve one that you do not believe even exists much less has the power to save you. Notice these verses say "to believe," which is complete faith and trust in the finished work of Jesus Christ. That means we cannot add or take anything away from what He has done; doing so is disobedience. Once you have followed the command to believe unto salvation, you are saved, a child of God, period. From that time forward out of a new and cleansed heart, a heart of love, we can and should glorify God in all that we do. Obedience is an outward action of what is on the inside, faith that produces action. This is what James talks about in James 2:18, "I'll show you my faith by my works."

Many of us today have a tendency to read our Bibles and choose which commands we want to obey and which ones we want to ignore. We decide that certain things are outdated and don't apply to us. We like to use the word *old-fashioned*. This is called incomplete obedience, which is none other than disobedience. King Saul found this out in 1 Samuel 15. God told Saul to go and to destroy the Amalekites because of their treatment of Israel after they came out of Egypt. He was to go and to destroy everything, wipe them completely out—destroy livestock, goods, people, destroy it all. Saul was victorious in battle. He destroyed everything, *but* he took the king prisoner. And he took all of the best livestock, the sheep and oxen, for himself. Later, he claimed he was going to sacrifice them to the Lord.

Saul was obedient in part of the mission, but he disobeyed before he finished the task. Saul, like many of us, did things his way rather than God's way, being partially obedient, which is disobedience. God was so angry with Saul he regretted making him king in the first place. God sent Samuel with a message to the king. And Samuel said,

> Hath the LORD as great delight in burnt offerings and sacrifices, as in obeying the voice of the LORD? Behold, to obey is better than sacrifice, and to hearken than the fat of rams. For rebellion is as the sin of witchcraft, and stubbornness is as iniquity and idolatry. Because thou hast rejected the word of the LORD, he hath also rejected thee from being king. (1 Sam. 15:22, 23)

Even if Saul had kept the livestock for the sole purpose of sacrifice, God would rather have obedience than all the sacrifices in the world. Many people want to sacrifice, perform rituals, and do good works by helping others. They never miss a church service. Yes, these are good things. These people are probably the nicest people you will ever meet, but they never obeyed the first command to believe. Salvation is through Jesus, not through our good deeds. "Believe on the Lord Jesus Christ and thou shalt be saved." One day that person will stand before Christ, and they will go down the list of the great things they have done. Christ will say, "Depart from me ye worker of iniquity. I never knew you. You lived a life of incomplete obedience, which is disobedience." Salvation is only through Jesus Christ and His finished work on the cross of Calvary. Believe on Him, and thou shalt be saved. When you are saved, then you will be able to serve.

Are you giving yourself completely over to the Lord?

> I beseech you therefore, brethren, by the mercies of God, that ye present your bodies a living sacrifice, holy, acceptable unto God, which is your reasonable service. And be not conformed to this world: but be ye transformed by the

renewing of your mind, that ye may prove what
is that good, and acceptable, and perfect, will of
God. (Rom. 12:1–2)

This verse reminds me of our brave American soldiers. I am
thankful how they have literally presented their bodies as a living
sacrifice for the freedoms we enjoy. From our forefathers to this present time, many have given their lives for the cause of freedom. Upon
joining the military, their lives no longer belong to themselves but
to the nation to serve. They are no longer conformed to civilian life
but are transformed through training into military warriors. Likewise
we, as Christians, are to present our bodies a living sacrifice to our
Lord and Savior Jesus Christ even unto death as many Christians
through the ages have willingly done for the cause of Christ. We are
in the world. We are not of the world; therefore, we shouldn't take
the shape or form of this world's lifestyle. But we are to be transformed by a continual renewing of our minds through the Word of
God and a close relationship with our Lord Jesus Christ, allowing
the Holy Spirit to control our lives. It's easy for us to get caught up
in materialism. We straddle the fence as we desire for ourselves, but
beware. Jesus says in Matthew 6:24,

No man can serve two masters: for either
he will hate the one, and love the other; or else
he will hold to the one, and despise the other. Ye
cannot serve God and mammon (money).

You have to ask yourself the question, am I serving God with a
servant's heart? Am I serving with the heart of a bird dog?

The servant worships, the servant obeys, and the servant has
a responsibility. We are His witnesses. Before Christ ascended into
heaven, He left his disciples with a task, also known as the Great
Commission.

Go ye therefore, and teach all nations, bap-
tizing them in the name of the Father, and of the

Son, and of the Holy Ghost: Teaching them to observe all things whatsoever I have commanded you: and, lo, I am with you always, even unto the end of the world. Amen. (Matt. 28:19–20)

Jesus said to go and tell what you know and what Christ has done in your life. Disciple or teach while you mature as a Christian. Take time to mentor other younger believers. Being a witness is not a onetime task. Being a witness is a lifestyle, literally meaning as you go or wherever you go.

I am reminded of my great-grandfather, who was an old-time country doctor. With horse and buggy, he would travel through town and over the countryside to deliver babies and help the sick. He had an office, located in town and open for set hours during the day, but he made house calls all through the night. He would sometimes sit late into the night with a feverish child or deliver a baby in the wee hours of the morning. Ol' Doc would then get his sleep while traveling on the long ride home since his horse knew the way. There was a wire stretched across the opening into the barn just high enough to catch my great-grandfather's hat as he went through. As the horse walked into the barn, the wire would knock the hat off his head and wake him up. He would then go inside and prepare for another day. He gave his life for the practice of medicine and to help others in need.

Just like the doctor, our Christian lives should be a continual witness. Everything we do is to bring glory to God and be a witness to others. We need to witness because the consequences are too great. Our family members, coworkers, and friends are watching everything we do. Tell them about Jesus and then show how He has changed your life by living it. What we do often has more of an impact than anything we could possibly say. Many times we think about telling someone about Jesus and put it off. We think, *Maybe I'll be a better witness later.* The problem is we might not have another chance because we never know what is around the next corner. That one could be taken away from here through death in a split second and spend eternity in hell, but you didn't tell them about Jesus Christ and what He has done for you.

I am reminded of a tragedy that happened many years ago. It was a rainy spring morning, May 9, 1980, when Capt. John Lerro was bringing a cargo ship, *The Summit Venture*, from the Gulf of Mexico into Tampa Bay. The *Summit Venture*, which was more than two hundred yards in length and weighed as much as twenty thousand tons. The rain started light that morning, but the storm began to strengthen and bring winds of more than 60 mph. With the rain coming down, visibility was nearly impossible. In fact, Capt. Lerro could not even see the bow of the ship. Even though he fought with all his might, the wind pushed the ship off course. The ship plowed into the Skyway Bridge pier; and a portion of the bridge, a scenic four-mile, 150-foot tall bridge, was sent into the water below. Capt. Lerro called out on the radio immediately, "Mayday! Mayday! Send emergency equipment! Stop traffic! The bridge is out!" A helpless Capt. Lerro called out in vain. It was too late. Without warning a Greyhound bus carrying 25 passengers plummeted 150 feet to their ultimate death. One by one, 6 more cars drove over the edge. Before it was over, 35 unsuspecting, innocent people lost their lives. Each woke up that morning headed out for just another day, not realizing they were headed to a road of destruction.[1]

If Capt. Lerro could somehow have stood at the edge of that bridge and stopped traffic to warn of the danger that was ahead, I'm sure he would have, but he didn't have a chance. Think how many of your friends and family members are on the broad road to destruction, not a physical but a spiritual road that will lead to eternal destruction and eternal punishment of hellfire that will never end. If you know the Word of God, you know the danger that lies ahead. Mayday! Mayday! Are you calling? Are you warning? Are you being the witness God would have you to be? Maybe you are not sure of your own salvation. Stop! Believe on the Lord Jesus Christ, and thou shalt be saved. How devastating it must have been for the families of those thirty-five people! What about those who didn't know the Lord Jesus Christ and His love for them? They had either rejected Him or

---

[1] "The Day the Skyway Fell," *St. Petersburg Times*; published May 7, 2000; Written by Jean Heller.

maybe they had never heard. Visibility was low that morning, and many drivers could barely see where they were going as they followed the vehicle in front of them. Satan has likewise blinded the minds of this world as they travel down the broad road of destruction. They cannot see what lies ahead; but it is up to you and me to tell them of Jesus, the Light of the world, and shine as lights. Only He can shine through the fog and open their eyes to salvation through the Holy Spirit.

God gave us tools to use for His glory: His word and prayer. We are to speak His words to the unsaved; live His words before the unsaved; and pray, pray, pray. God is not willing that any should perish but that all should come to repentance. James 5:16 also says that the effectual fervent prayer of a righteous man availeth much. This is that hot melting prayer of one who reads and lives the Word of God. This is the prayer of one pouring their heart and soul out to the Lord with all their being and then believing with all their heart, without a shadow of a doubt that God will answer. Isn't it worth it for that friend or loved one?

We, as Christians, need to be aware that we never look down upon that one to whom we are witnessing. Nothing is more detrimental to the work of the Lord. Remember you were a sinner before you were saved and you still battle with sin each day. In fact, you are a saved sinner, a beggar telling another beggar where to find bread. Have compassion, and show the love of Christ in your testimony with humility. Without love, your works are worthless. Be a witness. Don't try to change their lifestyle. Maddie is a dog, and dogs are dogs, no matter how many times we dress them up like humans. We talk to them as if they are our children and think they understand everything we say, but as soon as we turn our backs, they will roll in a dead animal carcass or drink out of the toilet and come and lick you in the face. That is their nature, and it cannot be changed. One who does not know Jesus Christ as Savior has a sin nature, and if you try to change them, you will only drive them further away. Only Jesus Christ can change the heart of a sinner through salvation and give them a new nature. I don't know about you, but when I was younger, I had a mouth that you might think I drank out of the toilet. But the Lord saved me, and then He changed me. We plant the seed and water the seed, but only God can give the increase. In other words, God will do the changing, just like He changed Paul's life and my life, and if you trust Him as Savior, He will change your life as well.

We see that serving God involves worship, obedience, and witness. Now the question is, Are you willing? Our abilities and talents are not important if we are willing to serve. Don't think for a second that you don't have what it takes. If you are willing, God will provide, meet your needs, and allow you to accomplish great things for His glory. Are you too small, too shy, or too weak? Look what Paul wrote in 1 Corinthians 1:27–29.

> But God hath chosen the foolish things of the world to confound the wise; and God hath chosen the weak things of the world to confound the things which are mighty; And base things of the world, and things which are despised, hath God chosen, yea, and things which are not, to bring to nought things that are: That no flesh should glory in his presence.

God has chosen the weak, the uneducated, the helpless, and the inadequate to carry out His plan so when the task is accomplished, there will be no doubt that God was in control all the way, therefore giving Him the glory that only He deserves.

Are you ashamed of your past and feel God can't use you? Did you know that God used a drunkard named Noah to preach God's judgment to a lost world and build an ark to save the human race as well as the animal kingdom from the great flood? Did you know God used a con man named Jacob to father His chosen people, Israel? Then there was Moses, a murderer and a man who couldn't speak plainly. God used Moses to lead His people out of the land of Egypt. Moses was also considered one of their greatest leaders. How about Rahab who ran a prostitution ring in Jericho? God used her to protect the spies? God used an adulterer and murderer named David to be the great king of Israel and promised his dynasty would be forever.

He used a coward named Jonah and a simple farmer named Amos as prophets to deliver His message. He used a hated unethical tax collector to be one of His disciples and to write the first gospel book in the New Testament. He used a man named Peter, a foul-mouthed fisherman, who continually put his foot in his mouth and denied the Lord three times before His crucifixion, to deliver the great message on the day of Pentecost, when three thousand souls fell down before God in repentance and trusted Jesus Christ as Savior in one day. Finally, He used a simpleminded country boy, shy and sinful, a used-car salesman who barely got a high school diploma, to write this book and to teach His Word. Any more questions? Any more doubts? If you are willing, get to work! God will use you.

Are you serving God in the capacity that He would have you to serve? Jesus promised that He would go away to provide a place for believers and He would return again to take those believers back to be with Him. We don't know the time in which He will return, but we do know that it will be when we least expect it. So the question is not when will He come but what will you be doing when He comes? Jesus said in Luke 12:37–40,

> Blessed are those servants, whom the lord when he cometh shall find watching: verily I say unto you, that he shall gird himself, and make them to sit down to meat, and will come forth and serve them. And if he shall come in the second watch, or come in the third watch, and find them so, blessed are those servants. And this know, that if the goodman of the house had known what hour the thief would come, he would have watched, and not have suffered his house to be broken through. Be ye therefore ready also: for the Son of man cometh at an hour when ye think not.

What will you be doing when the trumpet sounds? Will you be blessed or happy at His coming? Or will you be ashamed? There

57

will be many who will be embarrassed because they spent more time serving themselves rather than serving God. I heard a preacher once say, "We need to live like Christ died yesterday, arose this morning, and is coming back tomorrow."

God gave tools to accomplish His purposes. He gave His Word, and He gave the privilege of prayer, but on a more personal note, He gave gifts to each of us who are saved. Paul provides a list of gifts, but he gives the purpose of these gifts in Ephesians 4:11–12, "And he gave some, apostles; and some, prophets; and some, evangelists; and some, pastors and teachers; For the perfecting of the saints, for the work of the ministry, for the edifying of the body of Christ." Gifts are given to serve the Lord and to minister to one another, edifying and encouraging one another. God gives many gifts. There are people who have a gift of prayer. Some people have the gift of encouragement, and there are others with musical talents. Many people visit patients in hospitals or help others in various situations. Some people give their time by mowing the church yard and maintaining the grounds, and I could go on. The point is, God gave you a talent for a reason: to serve and to glorify Him with that talent.

I was saved at a fairly early age, and I have heard many messages on gifts and using them for God, but I had a problem in that I didn't know what my gift was. I looked around and saw other people and how they were gifted, but as for myself, I really had no clue. Being in business, I tried to use my trade as a way to glorify God, but that didn't seem to be enough. I woke up early one Monday morning in the fall of 2000 to have my devotion. I was in a rut as far as my spiritual life was concerned, and I was only going through the motions. As I sat down to read my Bible, I thought, *I need to study as if I'm going to teach this lesson.* Now understand I had no desire to teach, nor could I. I was too shy. Okay, let's face it, shy was an understatement. I would be scared to death! I remember the lesson well. It was the parable of the sower and the seed from Matthew 13. I studied all week, never telling anyone what I was doing. Then Saturday morning came. Out of the blue, I got a call from the Sunday school superintendent. He wanted to know if I would teach the junior boys class in the absence of their teacher. Of course, what else could I say?

Absolutely not! I could never do anything like that! So I politely declined, get someone else. As I hung up the phone, I was relieved. Whew! Glad that's over with, but no, the Lord wasn't finished. We had just built our house and planted grass down our fairly long driveway. That afternoon I got on my tractor to do a little work at the end of the driveway. As I drove along, I couldn't help but to notice how the grass was growing in patches. I thought, *There is the good ground where the grass is green, the hard rocky soil where the grass has been scorched by the sun, and then the places where the birds plucked up the seeds.* It was just like the lesson I had studied all week. I slammed on the brakes and thought, *If anyone can teach this lesson I can.* The Lord has put me in this position. If I fail, I fail, but I believe He will give me what I need to do His work. Needless to say, I have been teaching ever since, and what a blessing it has been.

I give you this testimony so that you might see that God has a plan and He has given you a gift to accomplish that plan. It may take a while to find what He has for you. But ask Him for guidance in the matter; wait on the Lord; and always, always be willing. We live in a society where everyone is entitled; it is the age of self and instant gratification. Our focus is continually on ourselves and what is best for us. Even in our prayers, as we go to the Lord, we ask for things, desires, wants, and needs. These are certainly things the Lord has asked us to do, and He will answer those prayers according to His will, but it is as if He is our servant rather than we being His servants. It's as if He is our genie in a bottle. Let me challenge you to go to the Lord in prayer, get your heart right with Him, and lay all your wants and desires aside. Just ask God, "What can I do for you? How can I serve you today?" He has given us so much. Can we not take time to give back to Him? This is part of living a Christ-centered life and being the servant God would have you to become.

Maddie continues to hold the point. She is honed in and focused like a laser on the task at hand, the purpose she was made to accomplish for her master, no matter what goes on around her as I walk up beside her. Imagine if we, as God's servants, could have that same focus on God's will and His purpose for our lives. We can only have that focus to accomplish His will with a servant's heart, the heart of a bird dog.

THE SHOTGUN

In order to become a successful bird hunter, it is important to have a good bird dog. It is equally important to have a good shotgun. At this present time, I am carrying a Franchi 20-gauge semiautomatic. I like the feel of this gun. It is lightweight, which suits well for these long hunts up and down the mountain. I also like the way the stock fits my cheekbone nice and tight and allows me to consistently put the gun in the same position each time I shoot. Of course, being consistent to my shooting position doesn't mean I'm consistent hitting the target. It seems here lately I have a bad case of the misses.

The shotgun is a tool, used to provide food for our family. It is also a weapon used for protection, and it brings pleasure to the hunter. As Maddie and I head out into the mountain, we are hunting for meat we can bring home to our family so that they might eat it for nourishment and growth. Thank the Lord for grocery stores. With the grouse population declining over the last several years in Southwest Virginia, if my family had to depend on me bringing grouse home for supper, we would all starve to death.

Just like the bird hunter needs a good shotgun, mankind needs the Word of God. As the shotgun provides food for our nourishment, the Word of God is that spiritual food providing nourishment to our souls. "And Jesus said unto them, I am the bread of life: he that cometh to me shall never hunger; and he that believeth on me shall never thirst" (John 6:35). Many people are hungering for satisfaction. There is an emptiness that cannot seem to be filled. Jesus is that life-giving bread. Only He can fill that emptiness, and we can only receive that life-giving bread by coming to Him and believing on Him. Once we receive Him as our Savior, we will never hunger or thirst, meaning we are saved to the uttermost and have eternal life through Jesus Christ our Lord.

Food gives our bodies nourishment for growth. When we are born into this world, our first desire is for food. We desire the milk from our mothers, and we cry until we receive that milk. In 1 Peter 2:2–3, we read, "As newborn babes, desire the sincere milk of the word, that ye may grow thereby: If so be ye have tasted that the Lord is gracious." The newborn baby desires milk; and when we are saved, or born again, into the family of God, we desire to learn and know more about our Savior and how He would have us to live in order to grow as Christians. This hunger is not the hunger to fill the emptiness that the unsaved person has but rather the hunger to know and desire a relationship with our Savior.

When Jesus says that He is "the bread of life," He is speaking of spiritual bread and spiritual hunger. Years ago I had a Brittany named Sophie, a beautiful liver-colored puppy. Rebecca wanted to keep her in the house. I didn't know anything about training an inside dog, but I was willing to give it a shot. After I stepped in a pile at the bottom of the steps one early morning and learned of her chewing the knobs on our nice antique furniture, I was about to give up on her and send her out to the pen with the other dog. Being a Brittany, she was a pleaser, and I honestly think she wanted to do the right thing. But like a lot of us, she just had a hard time doing so. Each night at bedtime, we would have devotions with the kids. Sophie would curl up on the bed and seem to listen as well. I don't remember the exact lesson; it must have been feeding on the Word of God. When I came home from work the next afternoon, she had literally eaten my daughter's new Bible. She had consumed most of the New Testament and left the rest in shavings. She was so proud of herself. She looked at me as if she had just saved Timmy from the mineshaft. After preaching her a sermon that kids didn't need to hear, she spent the next thirteen years in the dog pen.

Many of us, especially here in the land of plenty, eat three meals a day with snacks in between. I have to laugh many times when coworkers get to work shortly after they have had breakfast and say, "So what are we going to have for lunch?" We always seem to be craving the next meal, but spiritually, we seem to be satisfied with only one meal a week, Sunday morning service. We attend church services and rarely do we get much from that. We don't take our Bibles down and study them on our own. We don't seek the things of God for our personal lives. We don't desire the sincere milk of the Word, and we quickly become malnourished.

At no time in history has the Word of God been more plentiful and available, especially here in the United States of America. It is believed that more than five billion copies have been sold since the 1800s, making the Bible the most-sold book in history. We have no excuse! Many third world countries don't have the food to feed their people. We look at their children and how malnourished and susceptible to disease they are. Unfortunately, Christians in our day are malnourished from a lack of spiritual food, allowing sin and Satan to attack as a disease and bring them down and destroy their testimony before they ever get started.

Our church prayed for baby Noah for many months. Born with a rare condition called Russell-Silver syndrome, he was unable to gain any weight and nearly died several times. After many months of IVs, Noah graduated to a feeding tube. He is now eating solid foods. One in fifty thousand to one in one hundred thousand babies are born with this rare disorder. According to *Wikipedia*, these children will never grow to more than five feet tall. Babies with this syndrome are not interested in eating and consume only small amounts with difficulty.[2] I would say that 75 percent of Christians suffer spiritually from a similar type of disorder. Such Christians are not interested in feeding on the scriptures. Also, the small amounts they read are done with difficulty.

Paul realized that the Corinthians were not maturing and were not ready to move to the words with more substance. "I have fed you with milk, and not with meat: for hitherto ye were not able to bear it, neither yet now are ye able" (1 Cor. 3:2). The writer of Hebrews was also frustrated with the Hebrew Christians.

Of whom we have many things to say, and
hard to be uttered, seeing ye are dull of hearing.
For when for the time ye ought to be teachers,

---

[2] *Wikipedia*: Silver-Russell Syndrome (SRS).

> ye have need that one teach you again which be
> the first principles of the oracles of God; and
> are become such as have need of milk, and not
> of strong meat. For every one that useth milk is
> unskillful in the word of righteousness: for he is a
> babe. But strong meat belongeth to them that are
> of full age, even those who by reason of use have
> their senses exercised to discern both good and
> evil. (Heb. 5:11–14)

The baby is unskillful because he has a milk diet. I remember my grandfather Geney used to tell me, "Christopher, eat something that will stick to those ribs." The mature Christians feeding on the meat of the Word have the ability to take the Word and apply it to decisions they make in life. So the question is, Where are you as far as handling the Word of God? What are you feasting on? Are you growing as a Christian?

Just because there is plenty to eat doesn't mean that it's all good for us. We live in a day where processed foods are everywhere. Saturated fats, sodium, and sugar all lead to poor health and such things as clogged arteries, high blood pressure, and diabetes. In many cases, if we have a health problem, it is due to poor eating habits. We, as Christians, run into similar problems. Peter tells us to desire the sincere milk of the Word, and we desire everything but the Word. We spend hours in front of the television. According to studies, Americans spend nearly four hours a day watching television. American adults spend more than ten hours a day on electronic devices. If you throw in eight hours of sleep and a few hours of work, there is not much time to give back to the one who gave His life for us. Unfortunately, we feed on things that have no nutritional value, giving us a very unhealthy spiritual life, and we don't grow the way the Lord desires us to grow.

When I was about three or four years old, I would slip out to the barn and eat horse and mule feed. My parents couldn't figure out why my stomach was so big and the rest of me was so little. Turns out, the worms I was getting from the feed were stealing all the nutrients, and they were growing, but I wasn't. Many Christians are allowing the worms of _____ (you fill in the blank) to steal the nutrients of God's Word and letting Satan stunt their growth. Milk is the first step in the growth of the baby. Once the baby begins to grow, it needs more substance, solid foods that will allow the body to produce muscle and bone growth and the child to mature physically into a strong man or woman.

The shotgun helps provide food and is also used for protection. At any event where there is trouble, I can easily access a shotgun or other firearm and use it to protect me and my family. Fortunately, in our small town there is not much crime. In fact, we didn't start locking our doors until recently, and that's just because the pumpkins at the church down the road were stolen and it turned out that it was just a big black bear having a little fun. Even though I haven't had to use a shotgun to protect my family, I have had to use it to protect livestock. I remember when I was about thirteen years old. It was spring, and the sheep had already had their lambs, so we had a good-sized flock on the farm. Earlier in the afternoon, I had gotten home from school and was riding my bike. I managed to wipe out and put a gash in my knee. Several stiches were required. I went to bed fairly early that night, and as with many nights, my dad went to work around eleven. The moon was full, and everyone was asleep. With the pain from my leg, I tossed and turned. Suddenly out of the silence of the night came a scream that would raise the hair on the back of your neck. It sounded like the bloodcurdling scream of a woman, but it wasn't. It was a cat. I had never heard anything like it before, especially in our area. Before I could comprehend what it was, Mom came running in my room. The sheep! I quickly grabbed my shotgun and hobbled out into the night. The moon was so bright. It was almost like daytime. Fortunately, the sheep had already gathered in a pack near the barn, and thankfully, the cat never attacked. We sat there until daylight with shotgun in hand, waiting and listening as that thing moved back and forth on the ridge above us and screamed every few minutes until it faded into early morning silence. I didn't have to use the shotgun that night, but having sheep, I had to use it many other times when wild dogs would come down from time to time to have a feast of our flock.

Just like the shotgun protects, the Word of God teaches us about our protector and leads us to safety. In Ephesians 6, Paul writes about preparing the Christian soldier for battle with the armor of God for protection. Finally, he comes down to the weapon of the Christian soldier in verse 17: "And take the helmet of salvation, and the sword of the Spirit, which is the word of God." The writer of Hebrews tells us that "the word of God is sharper than any two-edged sword." One day the Lord will use His words in the judgment of this world.

> And I saw heaven opened, and behold a white horse; and he that sat upon him was called Faithful and True, and in righteousness he doth judge and make war. His eyes were as a flame of fire, and on his head were many crowns; and he had a name written, that no man knew, but he himself. And he was clothed with a vesture dipped in blood: and his name is called The Word of God. And the armies which were in heaven followed him upon white horses, clothed in fine linen, white and clean. And out of his mouth goeth a sharp sword, that with it he should smite the nations: and he shall rule them with a rod of iron: and he treadeth the winepress of the fierceness and wrath of Almighty God. (Rev. 19:11–15)

We are reminded of the power of the Word of God. One day He will destroy the nations just by speaking, and the blood will run as deep as a horse's bridle. This is the power of our protector. As we protect ourselves with guns and other weapons, we will eventually run out of ammunition. Peter tells us,

> For all flesh is as grass, and all the glory of man as the flower of grass. The grass withereth,

and the flower thereof falleth away: But the word of the Lord endureth forever. And this is the word which by the gospel is preached unto you. (1 Pet. 1:24–25)

Throughout history, God has protected His people. Although He judged the world by the flood, He protected the seed of Adam through Noah and the ark. Before He destroyed Sodom and Gomorrah, God made sure there was no righteous man left. He led Lot and his family out before fire came down from heaven and consumed the cities. He promised Abraham that He would make his seed a great nation. Even through captivity, slavery, and brutal murders, God has continued to watch over that nation; and He will one day rule and reign from the very city of Jerusalem. He protected such individuals as David, Daniel, Shadrach, Meshach, and Abednego, to name a few. He even promised to protect those of us who believe on the Lord Jesus Christ. I am reminded of Psalm 23, where we read about the Lord being our Shepherd: "Yea, though I walk through the valley of the shadow of death, I will fear no evil: for thou art with me; thy rod and thy staff they comfort me" (Ps. 23:4). The Lord never said we would escape hard times, but He did say He would be with us all the way. Jesus said, "I will never leave you nor forsake you."

David lived in difficult times. As a young shepherd boy, he had to protect himself and his sheep from lions and bears. As he got a little older, he stood up against Goliath and killed him with one smooth stone that he threw from a sling. Later, Saul, the king of Israel, tried numerous times to kill him or trap him in some way. Each time David traveled through the valley of the shadow of death, and the Lord was with him. The great Shepherd's rod and staff comforted him all the way, and when he climbed out on the other side, the Lord made him the greatest king Israel had ever known. No wonder David described the Lord as the horn of his salvation, his rock, high tower, shield, strength, refuge and shepherd, the great Shepherd who laid His life down for His sheep and will one day return to gather them up again. What a comfort to know that our Lord is with us all the way! He is our protector. The Word of God gives us these words of comfort: that nothing can separate us from the love of God. Our Lord Jesus Christ told us that nothing can pluck us out of the Father's hand.

The shotgun brings pleasure. I enjoy getting out and shooting clay pigeons. Sometimes my sons will come out and shoot as well. With our busy schedules, it opens the door for fellowship, a time to talk with each other. And yes, it is always a competition, and somehow I end up getting skunked.

One day I was out shooting and working on my right-to-left swing. I was in a slump and couldn't seem to hit anything. My youngest son, Tate, came out to pull for me. As he pulled time after time, he continued to laugh at my shooting ability and tell me how it was supposed to be done—oh yeah, and how he was a lot better than me. Finally, I gave in. "Okay, bud, let's see what you've got." One by one, he smoked each of them. I had to eat a little crow, but we still had an enjoyable time. I had to once again learn to swallow my pride.

Knowing from the Word of God that God is our provider and protector gives us comfort, which brings joy to our lives. Joy fills our hearts as we learn and fellowship with our Father in heaven through study and prayer. As we read our Bibles, He speaks to us; and as we pray, we speak to Him, giving us that much needed fellowship and creating a loving relationship with the one who saved us from our sins. This gives us pleasure, the unspeakable joy of a father and his child. I am reminded of the words of the psalmist in Psalm 119:103, "How sweet are thy words unto my taste! yea, sweeter than honey to my mouth!" God's words bring joy and satisfaction.

John wrote the Gospel of John late in his life, many years after Christ had ascended into heaven. Many false prophets had come on the scene and were deceiving the people as well as those young Christians. There was much uncertainty in their lives, which brings fear and doubt. It is impossible to live a joyful life as long as fear is ruling our lives. John wrote the gospel so "that we might know that Jesus is the Christ the son of God, and that believing ye might have life through his name." He also went on to write the Epistles "that your joy may be full." Our God, our Father in heaven, desires the best for each of us. He also desires that we be joyful. By knowing His

Word and obeying His words, we can be confident and grow in His grace and knowledge thereby making us perfect or mature. "All scripture is given by inspiration of God (this literally means God-breathed or spoken)" (2 Tim. 3:16–17). God moved on the hearts of the men to write His words, to speak to you and me. "And it is profitable for doctrine, for reproof, for correction, for instruction in righteousness: That the man of God may be perfect, thoroughly furnished unto all good works." As the Word of God nourishes our souls and we grow to perfection or maturity as Christians, we can rejoice in the Lord, no matter what we are going through in our lives. Through maturity, we can borrow the words of Habakkuk: "Yet I will rejoice in the LORD, I will joy in the God of my salvation" (Hab. 3:18).

A good hunter knows his gun and knows it well. Basic knowledge is important for the success of the hunter. There are many different styles of shotguns on the market today: automatics, single shots, pumps, and double barrels. Finding a gun that fits well and the gauge you prefer (generally 12 and 20 gauge are the most popular) is very important. Each gun is designed to shoot a certain pattern. The patterns are adjusted by the choke, located at the end of the barrel where the shot exits. There are four basic chokes: cylinder, improved cylinder, modified, and full. Cylinder, or open, allows the shot to spread into a wider pattern, which is good for shooting such fast-moving targets as the ruffed grouse. The full choke shoots a tighter, more accurate pattern, needed for shooting such game as a spring gobbler. Some chokes are built into the barrel from the factory; others are interchangeable or adjustable. The hunter must know what pattern the shotgun is shooting before he goes hunting. Also important is the ammunition. There are many types of shells and shot, including high brass, low brass, 8 shot, all the way down to 4 shot. We use 7 1/2 shot on grouse in the fall and for greater penetration, maybe 6s in the cold of winter. When hunting turkeys, we would use 4 or 6 shot. The lower the number, the larger the shot. The larger the shot, the fewer the number of pellets in the shell. There are a few simple things the hunter must know about the gun he is using: how to load it, where the safety is and how it works, and where the sight and trigger are located. These things seem so simple. I shouldn't need to mention them, but they are basic foundation to the shooter. The simple foundation of the Word of God is that God created the heavens and the earth, we are sinners and need a Savior, and Jesus loves us and died for our sins and arose on the third day. These statements seem so simple, but we need to be reminded of these truths constantly.

Knowing the shotgun is an important key to success for the hunter. Knowing the Word of God is an important key to success for the Christian. "Study to shew thyself approved unto God, a workman that needeth not to be ashamed, rightly dividing the word of truth" (2 Tim. 2:15).

The Word of God tells us of a loving God in order that we learn about Him and know He created all things for Himself and that everything is about him and not about you and me, regardless of what is taught in schools today. It's about Jesus first; others second; and yourself last, which is that lifestyle and acronym that spells JOY. Through the Word of God, we know His righteousness, and we see He is perfect and holy. We learn that we are sinners from Adam, and no one can deny that our hearts are continually wicked if we are honest with ourselves. Through the Word of God, we learn of His love, mercy, and grace, in that while we were yet sinners Christ died for each and every one of us and that, believing, we might be saved. Finally, we learn how to serve the Lord through examples from the patriarchs all the way to the apostles and many other leaders of history. We know the beginning and the ending and that when we put our faith and trust in Him as our Savior, one day we will be in His very presence for all eternity.

Basic knowledge of the shotgun is a necessity to the hunter, but without practice, it is useless. By practicing regularly, the hunter truly gets to know the gun, not just know about the gun. Some targets will not be moving; they will be standing still. Others will be moving, some faster than others. The elusive ruffed grouse is one of the most difficult birds I have ever hunted. The bird takes off flying with the sound of thunder, which startles you if you're not ready, and moves at the speed of a fighter jet, most of the time disappearing as fast as it appeared. You only have a split second to shoot, so practice is essential.

The shotgun has a safety, trigger, and sight. The hunter spends time picking a spot on the wall and bringing the gun from the carrying position to the shooting position. He practices removing the safety and aiming at the target in one smooth motion so as soon as the sight covers the target, the gun is ready to fire. The objective is to get the feel of the gun and know it so well that you don't have to look at the safety, trigger, or even the sight. Because when the bird gets up, there is absolutely no time. Skeet shooting and clay pigeons are the best practices for the bird hunter. The hunter should be able to shoot from left to right, right to left, over his head, or even going straight away, any direction a bird could possibly fly. Practice makes perfect, so practice perfectly, and when that grouse takes off, you will have an opportunity to take the bird.

Believers need to know the Word of God and practice the Word of God in their lives.

> But sanctify the Lord God in your hearts:
> and be ready always to give an answer to every
> man that asketh you a reason of the hope that is
> in you with meekness and fear. (1 Pet. 3:15)

There is nothing more frustrating than to get a quick point and then the bird flushes while I've got my hands in my pockets or I'm not paying attention and not ready to shoot. Always be ready! It's amazing how opportunities come along. You get a few minutes to talk to a friend about Jesus Christ, and you aren't ready. You have a split second to say the right thing to keep the conversation going, and you stand silent or change the subject. Once the moment has passed, it's gone. You can never get it back. Just like the ol' grouse, it flushed, and you had your hands in your pockets. Take the Word of God, and learn it, touch it, feel it, know it. Put it to practice in your own life, and be ready. Opportunities will arise.

Every successful hunter must have confidence or faith in his shotgun, being sure of the equipment, both from knowledge and practice. Just like a basketball player standing at the free throw line, confidence equals success. Through study of the Word of God and spiritual growth, our confidence, or faith, grows in our God and in His precious words and promises. The Holy Spirit will give us confidence to accomplish His will. We can make Philippians 4:13 personal and say, "I can do all things through Christ which strengtheneth me." Through the Word of God, we know that God knows our needs even before we know or even ask; therefore, we can "come boldly to the throne of grace."

The success of the hunter depends on his or her focus. The hunter must focus on the target and bring the gun to the target; there is no time to aim. This is a form of instinctive shooting. The basketball player doesn't focus on the ball while he is shooting. The focus is on the back of the rim. The baseball pitcher focuses on the catcher's mitt, and the batter focuses on the ball. Now think about the Word of God. Throughout the Old Testament, there are many pictures and types, each one pointing to Christ. He is the focus. The prophets prophesied of the coming Christ, who would come to die for our sins and also rule and reign over the world. The good news of the gospels is written so we might know Christ came to die for the sins of the world and arise again on the third day, fulfilling the prophecies and proving that the price for our sins was paid. By faith in the finished work, we have eternal life. The letters to the churches and the Epistles were written so we might handle ourselves well and live our lives pleasing to our Lord Jesus Christ. Finally, the book of Revelation was written to reveal Jesus Christ, His coming judgment on this sinful world, and His return to reign forever and ever. He is the focus of the Word of God. He is the Word of God. It is all about Him; therefore, we need to keep our eyes on our wonderful Lord and Him only.

As a young boy, I remember hunting with my father and grandfather. It was the day after Thanksgiving, and we were hunting along a creek bottom on the edge of a cornfield. As we came up on a large grove of briars, the dogs pointed. Being the youngest of the three generations, I was designated to go in for the kill. I began to ease in behind the pointing dogs, and as I walked past, twenty-five to thirty quail flew up all at once. Some flew in a group; others singled out and went in different directions. I aimed right in the middle of the large group. *Bang! Bang!* They were all safe; not one fell out of the sky. How could I have missed? They were right in front of me. Granddad laughed, and he said, "Son, do you know why you missed those birds?" I just grinned. "No, sir." He explained, "You were focused on the whole covey, too many at one time. Pick one bird, focus on that one, and shoot. Then you can move to another." Words of wisdom! Sometimes I need to hear those words again. With so many things going on in our lives, I don't know about you, but sometimes I feel like a cat with nine tails. It is so easy to get caught up in the daily activities that we neglect the most important one in our lives: the Lord Jesus Christ. When it comes to Bible study, our focus is also too broad. We read the Bible through in a year, reading three or four chapters a day and call that our devotion time and move on to the next thing in our busy schedules. I know pastors who read the Bible through a couple of times a year. These readings give a perspective of the Bible as a whole. They help to keep things in context from beginning to end. Unfortunately, these reading times are also used as devotion times. How much do you really get out of reading three chapters in twenty minutes, and you're done? Yes, you are shooting at three birds at one time, and you are probably going to miss the point. It's hard to apply that much to your life so that you might grow. If you are going to read the Bible through in a year, that's fine, but have a separate devotion time. Take one verse, one chapter, one passage; and focus on that one. Pray about it, ask the Lord for understanding, learn it, understand it, meditate on it, and then apply that verse or chapter to your life so that you might grow as a servant of God. With this focus and devotion, you will hit the target every time.

When the storms begin to brew all around us, we are often not sure where to turn. Panic sets in, and our hearts are fearful. Uncertainty rules our lives, and our focus is blurred. Matthew tells the story of Jesus walking on water and Peter's weak faith. To paraphrase (Matthew 14:22–36), it was one stormy night on the Sea of Galilee. The disciples were fearful for their lives. The winds were howling, and the boat was being tossed to and fro. The disciples faced certain shipwreck and death. As they looked out over the water, they saw Jesus walking toward them. At first they thought they saw a ghost, but they soon realized it was Jesus. Peter called out to the Lord, "If it is you, Lord, bid me come out there that I might walk on the water." Peter began to take that first step of faith as he stepped out onto the sea. He looked down at the water and then at Jesus. He took another step and another. He was doing well until the winds began to blow harder and the waves grew higher. It was then that Peter was focused on the many circumstances rather than the one solution, the Lord Jesus Christ, and he began to sink.

Maybe you are in a difficult situation. The waves are crashing around you. Where is your focus? Is it on the Lord or the many problems? Our Lord has promised, "I will never leave you nor forsake you." When we focus on the Lord, we see His great power and realize our problems are nothing in His sight and that He will see us through them, so keep your eyes on the Lord. Take it one step at a time and one day at a time. You can then handle trials with joy, as you have hit the mark and are living a life of perfection, or maturity, to the glory of our Lord.

The shotgun is a tool. Designed to kill, the shotgun needs to be handled with respect. When I was growing up, my father told me more than once, "A gun knows no friends." Accidents happen every year in the US. Kids get their hands on guns and don't have a clue what they are doing or how dangerous they are. Grown-ups carry guns and use them carelessly. Knowing the danger, I had my kids carry an empty shotgun their first year of hunting so they would safely learn how to handle a gun. Hunter safety is so important. Why turn an enjoyable time into a tragedy? Sometimes, no matter how careful we are, we can still have accidents.

A few years ago, as grouse season was winding down, probably in early February, I was hunting along a hillside when I came to a small stream. It appeared Maddie was pointing, so I had to move quickly. The weather had been cold the previous two weeks, and we had been in a deep freeze, so the ground was frozen solid. On this day, the sun was shining bright, and the temperatures were in the upper thirties, so things were beginning to thaw. When the ground is frozen underneath and thawing on top, it makes for some really slick conditions, as "slick as a pealed onion," you might say. As I moved down, my feet slipped out from under me, and I wiped out. I normally laugh at things like this, but this time as I was falling, I let go of my shotgun. It landed on the stock and fell back toward me with the barrel pointing right at my face. As I got up, I noticed the safety had been knocked off, and it was ready to fire. *What if?* That was all I could think. Though a little shaken, I had to thank the Lord for sparing me one more time.

The Word of God is like a sharp two-edged sword that must be handled with utmost care.

> For the word of God is quick, and powerful,
> and sharper than any two-edged sword, piercing
> even to the dividing asunder of soul and spirit,
> and of the joints and marrow, and is a discerner of
> the thoughts and intents of the heart. (Heb. 4:12)

The Word of God cuts and convicts. My father always told me a gun knows no friends. Our God is no respecter of persons. How many times have I looked to use the Word of God to convict someone else and the Lord shot me through the heart and caused me to repent of my own sin?

God's Word can also be detrimental if not used properly. "Study to shew thyself approved unto God a workman that needeth not to be ashamed, rightly dividing the word of truth" (2 Tim. 2:15). The key phrase is "rightly dividing the word," prayerful consideration of what the Lord is saying to us and keeping things in context. Many false prophets attempt to make the Bible say the things they want to hear, deceiving many and leading them to an eternal death. John warns to "beware of ravenous wolves, deceivers," people who handle the word carelessly and are dangerous to all with whom they come in contact. Remember 2 Timothy 3:16, which states all scripture is given by inspiration of God, literally God-breathed. Hebrews 12:29 reminds us that our God is a "consuming fire." God is to be reverenced and respected. He is holy, and his Word is holy. James warns teachers, knowing that they shall receive a greater condemnation.

> For I testify unto every man that heareth the words of the prophecy of this book, If any man shall add unto these things, God shall add unto him the plagues that are written in this book: And if any man shall take away from the words of the book of this prophecy, God shall take away his part out of the book of life, and out of the holy city, and from the things which are written in this book. (Rev. 22:18–19)

After falling with my shotgun that day, I realized I needed to learn how to fall with my gun in my hand, not only for my protection, but also for others. Now when I walk in treacherous places, most of the time I unload it. Otherwise, I hold my gun tight to my chest. I make sure the safety is on and both my hands are away from the trigger, so if I fall, the gun stays tight against me, and I don't let go. In the Christian walk, there will be times when we stumble and maybe even fall, but we need to learn how to fall. We need to learn how to take the Word of God and hold it tight to our hearts and when we stumble to never let go. I am reminded of the words of David: "Thy word have I hid in mine heart, that I might not sin against thee" (Ps. 119:11). Hide God's Word, and hold it close.

One who handles the Word of God improperly can send a person to hell for eternity. One who uses it properly can bring salvation and eternal life. One can be a stumbling block to a young Christian or an encourager, lifting one up. A person can be led astray into the depths of destruction or led in the paths of righteousness where one can have joy unspeakable. Take the Word of God for what it says. Don't try to spin it to make you feel better. The Word of God is a two-edged sword, and it's supposed to cut. God gave His Word for a reason and a purpose. Apply it to your life for doctrine, reproof, correction, and instruction in righteousness so that you might be mature and thoroughly furnished unto all good works, as Paul tells us in second Timothy.

When the old shotgun hangs over the fireplace mantel, its only purpose is for decoration. It collects dust, and if you needed to use it, all the parts would be so rusty it wouldn't even fire. The old family Bible sits on the coffee table, and it is only opened on occasion to make sure you don't forget your anniversary. The Bible is so full of information, the very keys to eternal life found all through the pages. It's the story of a loving God. Oh, how He loved his creation! The good news of the gospel and how He sent His son to die for our sins fills the pages, and yet it lays there only for decoration. It is as useless as the old gun on the mantle. In fact, if you are not using the Word of God in your life, you might as well be hunting without a gun.

Jesus said, "Seek, and ye shall find." Let me challenge you. Pick up that old dusty Bible, and wipe it off. Go hunting for the Creator, go hunting for His salvation and His wisdom, and go hunting for the truth.

THE POWERS OF THE AIR

After a few hours of hunting, it's getting about time for a break. We climb a large rock and sit down to take in all the scenery. It is a breathtaking view, especially since I'm scared of heights. The large valley below is surrounded by a blue mountain range that seems to go on forever. I kick back to enjoy some of Rebecca's homemade lunch that she prepared before I left home. Maddie muzzles up against me and looks at me with those sad brown eyes, thinking she is going to get some as well. I rub her soft head and tell her, "I'll give you a pat, but you ain't gettin' my lunch." After lunch, I continue to take in the view. In the distance, I hear the screech of a red-tailed hawk. A few minutes go by as the hawk comes into sight. With his large majestic wings, he glides along effortlessly through the sky. I am amazed at his beauty as the sun reflects off his red tail and large gray wings. He glides gracefully around in circles and seeks his prey. Suddenly without warning, he pulls his wings in tight. Like a rock, he falls out of the sky. At the last second, before he hits the ground, he spreads his wings and, with his talons extended, reaches out to grab his innocent prey.

I am reminded of 1 Peter 5:8, "Be sober, be vigilant; because your adversary the devil, as a roaring lion, walketh about, seeking whom he may devour." Our adversary is watching, waiting to pounce on his prey. So always be ready and pay attention, because as soon as we put our guard down, he will reach out with his talons to devour. It is Satan's desire to devour and destroy everything that God has created. Satan is our opponent or adversary. Before battling our opponent, we must know and understand him and his tactics. The name Satan actually means adversary, or opponent. Satan has many other names as well. Before his fall, he was named Lucifer, the son of the morning. After the fall, he was named Satan, or adversary. But he is also called the devil, the dragon, the god of this world, and the prince of the power of the air, to name a few. Some people view Satan as a fictional character with horns and a pitchfork. Others actually worship Satan. Some people fear him. They know that he is evil, but he is controlling their lives through deception.

Satan is a created being. He was created by God for the glory of God. Ezekiel describes Satan before the fall. God had a message for the king of Tyrus. This king was so evil that the Lord spoke to him as if he was Satan himself, because Satan was behind him and was influencing and controlling every step he took.

> Moreover the word of the LORD came unto me, saying, Son of man, take up a lamentation upon the king of Tyrus, and say unto him, Thus saith the Lord GOD; Thou sealest up the sum, full of wisdom, and perfect in beauty. Thou hast been in Eden the garden of God; every precious stone was thy covering, the sardius, topaz, and the diamond, the beryl, the onyx, and the jasper, the sapphire, the emerald, and the carbuncle, and gold: the workmanship of thy tabrets and of thy pipes was prepared in thee in the day that thou wast created. Thou art the anointed cherub that covereth; and I have set thee so: thou wast upon the holy mountain of God; thou hast walked up and down in the midst of the stones of fire. Thou wast perfect in thy ways from the day that thou wast created, till iniquity was found in thee. (Ezek. 28:11–15)

Satan was one of God's greatest and most beautiful creatures. Notice the beautiful and valuable stones with which he was covered. He was the great anointed angel who stood before God. As great and as beautiful as Satan was, he was still a created being, created by the eternal, Almighty God; however, Satan allowed pride to fill his heart. Verse 17 continues, "Thine heart was lifted up because of thy beauty, thou hast corrupted thy wisdom by reason of thy brightness: I will cast thee to the ground, I will lay thee before kings, that they may behold thee."

Isaiah states,

> How art thou fallen from heaven, O Lucifer, son of the morning! How art thou cut down to the ground, which didst weaken the nations! For thou hast said in thine heart, I will ascend into heaven, I will exalt my throne above the stars of God: I will sit also upon the mount of the congregation, in the sides of the north: I will ascend above the heights of the clouds; I will be like the most high. (Isa. 14:12–14)

Satan in his pride, as his heart was lifted up, proclaimed that he would be like the Most High. Being the greatest of creation was not enough for Satan. He wanted to be worshipped above God. So God, who is holy and righteous and perfect in all things, the only one who is worthy of worship, cast Satan out of His presence. We see in Revelation 12:4a that he took one-third of the angels with him. "And his tail drew the third part of the stars of heaven, and did cast them to the earth…" From that time, Satan has been out to destroy. When God created the earth and everything in it, Satan was watching, and when God created Adam and Eve in his own image, Satan was ready to pounce and deceive Eve and to cause her to sin against God.

Unlike God, Satan is a created being, but he is also a spirit. Because he is a spirit, he has no borders as we would. He has no body to become weary or wear out and die, but remember, Satan is only one. God is all-powerful, all-present, and all-knowing. Although Satan is powerful, he is not all-powerful; although he is present, he is not all-present; and although he knows much, he is not all-knowing. In fact, he cannot even be compared to God. Needless to say, Satan has plenty of help as one-third of the angels who fell are with him. These are demons setting out to wreak havoc on mankind by possessing, influencing, and causing men to do things that are unseemly.

This is the spiritual warfare that every person encounters through-out their lives. Since we are born with a sin nature, our hearts and desires are evil continually, so we cannot blame Satan for all our sins. Many of our choices are to satisfy the sin nature, or the flesh. Being sinners makes us enemies of God. As Christians, being born again, we still have that sin nature; and many times we allow that nature to have its way in disobedience to our God on our own. Satan and his angels influence our lives. They know our weaknesses, and they bring things into our lives to keep us from serving God. Satan has also blinded the minds of this world, keeping the unsaved from under-standing the glorious gospel of Christ. Also, he and his army seek to destroy the testimony of Christians and cause them to fall, making the message of no effect. As the day draws closer to Satan's ultimate defeat, he is leading the charge of a great falling away, a time where many are turning away from the truth and therefore believing a lie. These things will allow Satan to set up a one-world system where the Antichrist will rule the world until the Lord Jesus Christ returns to destroy him and his army.

Although Satan is powerful and mighty in our eyes, he is only a created being and cannot overcome his Creator. We are comforted by the words of 1 John 4:4b, "Greater is he that is in you, than he that is in the world." When we trust Jesus Christ as our Savior, the Holy Spirit indwells us. The Holy Spirit is the third person of the Godhead, and He is greater than Satan. Not only is Satan inferior to God, he is also in subjection to God. We learn this in the book of Job. To paraphrase Job 1:6–7, we see a time when the angels come before God to give an account for the things they had done. Satan also comes before God. God asks Satan where he had been, and his reply is that he had been going to and fro in the earth and walking up and down it, seeking whom he may devour. God asks Satan if he considered his servant Job, who was an upright and righteous man. In reply, Satan says to the Lord, "If you take away all the bless-ings that you have given him, he will curse you to your face." God then gives Satan permission to remove all the blessings, right down to destroying Job's own children, but God is still in control as he tells Satan in verse 12, "You can take these blessings, but you cannot harm Job." Satan is in complete subjection. Again in chapter 2, Satan returns after failing to destroy Job. The Lord once again asks him, "Have you considered my servant Job?" Satan replies, "If you take his health, he will curse you to your face." Once again, God allows Satan to attempt to destroy Job by covering his entire body with painful boils, yet God tells Satan that he cannot take Job's life. Satan can only do what God allows. God is in complete control while Satan is in complete subjection.

Satan has many weapons at his disposal, besides outright destruction, as he used on Job. These weapons are used to keep unsaved people from accepting the good news of the gospel of Christ, leading them to an eternity of destruction. They are also used to destroy or cause Christians to stumble so they will be of no use to the Savior. These three weapons in particular are deception, doubt, and distraction.

Satan's number one weapon is deception. While speaking to the Pharisees, Jesus says in John 8:44,

> Ye are of your father the devil, and the lusts
> of your father ye will do. He was a murderer
> from the beginning, and abode not in the truth,
> because there is no truth in him. When he spea-
> keth a lie, he speaketh of his own: for he is a liar,
> and the father of it.

In John 14:6, Jesus says, "I am way, the truth, and the life: no man cometh unto the Father, but by me." Plain and simply put, Jesus proclaims the way to God, the way to eternal life in heaven. Since Jesus is the way to the Father, there is no other way to the Father. Since Jesus is the truth, then everything else is a lie. Since Jesus is the life, everything else is dead. Remember Satan said that he would be "like God" in Isaiah 14. He couldn't be God; he could only attempt to be like God because he is a created being. It is Satan's desire to be worshipped above God. Satan is an imitator. His plan is to counterfeit or distort the truth, deceiving people into believing there is more than one way. When a counterfeiter makes a $20 bill, he makes it as close to the real thing as possible so he can pass it off as the real thing, yet it is still a counterfeit.

Speaking of deception, years ago, the old-timers were sitting around the campsite, listening to the fox hounds run. They were always telling jokes and playing tricks on one another. There was a man named Percy, who set himself up for a classic prank. He slipped away to the bathroom, which was an old oak tree a few yards back. While he was gone, my grandfather quickly pulled out a can of Alpo canned dog food and poured it in a bowl. When Percy returned, Granddad made quite a fuss over how well my grandmother Francis's "beef stew" tasted. Of course, ol' Percy had to check it out for himself. He took a small taste at first and then another spoonful. With a grin on his face and licking his lips, Percy replied, "Chris, that's the best beef stew I ever had! Tell Francis to give that recipe to my wife." While Satan tries to deceive us, we need to seek the truth. The bank teller knows a $20 bill so well that when a counterfeit is presented, the teller automatically detects it, and if Percy had ever had any of my grandmother's beef stew, he would have known that it was a counterfeit.

If we know Jesus Christ as the way, the truth, and the life, we will not be deceived and led astray. When Jesus made this statement, He began with "I Am." That was one of the seven "I Am" statements in the book of John. For example, "I Am the light of the world," and "I Am the bread of life." "I Am" is a statement proclaiming God's deity, who He really is: God in the flesh. He is the visible, making known the invisible. This was the same "I Am" statement that God used in Exodus while talking to Moses. John began his gospel by proclaiming that Jesus Christ is God. "In the beginning was the Word" (John 1:1). The beginning is eternity past because God has no beginning. Jesus Christ is the Word. "The Word was with God." This is the eternal perfect fellowship: God the Father, God the Son, and God the Holy Spirit. Finally, "the Word was God," plain and simple. Verse 3 goes on to tell of creation. The Word was there, all things were made by Him, and nothing was made without Him. Verse 14 states that "the word was made flesh and dwelt among us." John was an eyewitness. It is hard for us to understand because we can only be one. Satan can only be one; but God is three in one, three persons of the Godhead, the Father, the Son, and the Holy Spirit. St. Patrick preached all over his homeland teaching the Trinity by using a three-leaf clover. The clover has three leaves, yet it is still one. Now I have to say, I still cannot fathom this with my simple, little mind. God never told us to understand, but He told us to simply believe. The late Vance Havner once said, "I don't understand electricity, but that doesn't mean I'm going to sit in the dark trying to figure it out."

Throughout Old Testament history, men went before God making animal sacrifices to cover their sins so that they might have fellowship with God. Each animal had to be without blemish. In other words, the animal could not be sick or maimed. It had to be in perfect health, picturing the ultimate sacrifice that was to come, the perfect Lamb of God. Each of these sacrifices covered the sins of the people. These sins were never paid for, only covered. Jesus Christ came to be that perfect sacrifice that would pay in full the sins of the world. Since man could not live a perfect life, God Himself had to take on a human body. As only God can be perfect, so Jesus Christ had to be fully God in order to be perfect, but He had to be fully man to die on the cross for our sins.

> But we see Jesus, who was made a little lower than the angels for the suffering of death, crowned with glory and honour; that he by the grace of God should taste death for every man. For it became him, for whom are all things, and by whom are all things, in bringing many sons unto glory, to make the captain of their salvation perfect through sufferings. (Heb. 2:9–10)

Any teaching that says Jesus Christ was just a man is a counterfeit and is antichrist. John warns us that anyone that teaches that Jesus Christ did not come in the flesh is the spirit of antichrist.

> Beloved, believe not every spirit, but try the spirits whether they are of God: because many false prophets are gone out into the world.

> Hereby know ye the Spirit of God: Every spirit that confesseth that Jesus Christ is come in the flesh is of God: And every spirit that confesseth not that Jesus Christ is come in the flesh is not of God: and this is that spirit of antichrist, whereof ye have heard that it should come; and even now already is it in the world. (1 John 4:1–3)

Anti means against. If it is against Christ, it is pro, or with, Satan. It is a counterfeit and the wrong way. Jesus is the Christ, the only way to salvation and the Father.

Another of Satan's tactics is doubt. Generally, when we begin to doubt ourselves and our salvation, fear will set in. Doubt and fear go hand in hand. When Jesus was hanging on the cross of Calvary and before He gave up the ghost, He cried out, "It is finished!" The perfect sacrifice has been made, and the price for the sins of man has been paid. Because of doubt, there are many people who are led to believe they need something else, whether it is good works, baptism, or some other ritual. Jesus said, "It is finished!" He has made the sacrifice, and He has paid it all.

If God, being perfect, made the perfect sacrifice, then what can I do to add to it? Think about it. Are you so great that you can top or add to what Christ has done? This is pride! As a sinner, I am in debt up to my eyeballs. I cannot even make the first payment for my sins, but Jesus paid it all. He paid it in full, and He gave salvation as a gift to you and me. So do you believe and receive the gift, or do you doubt and reject the gift? "For the wages of sin is death; but the gift of God is eternal life through Jesus Christ our Lord" (Rom. 6:23). A gift is not earned; it is received. If one teaches that salvation is anything other than a gift to receive from God, then it is a counterfeit and false teaching from Satan and his angels. Satan has blinded the minds of many people, so they think they have secured a home in heaven, but they are completely lost. Rather than putting their full faith and trust in the Lord Jesus Christ, they doubt what He has done for them and are headed for eternal punishment for their sins. Oh, if only you would believe! There are also Christians who struggle with doubts of salvation. Being saved at an early age can be difficult because you don't see the change in your life that, for example, an alcoholic or someone who lived a wicked lifestyle would see when they trusted Christ and He completely changed their lives. Doubts come into our minds, and we question, "Did I really trust Christ as my Savior?" These doubts bring fear. It could be a fear that causes us to no longer serve the Lord because we aren't sure if we were ever saved or a fear that keeps us up at night and leads us to worry and ask, "If I died tonight, where would I spend eternity?"

Fear in the Bible is used in two ways. In Proverbs 1:7, it is stated that the fear of the Lord is the beginning of knowledge. This fear is a reverential respect for God. God is holy, and God is worthy of our respect and worship. Realizing who God is opens our eyes to knowledge, and we reverence Him. This a godly fear. The other fear is a paralyzing fear. Second Timothy 1:7 tells us that "the spirit of fear is not of God." This paralyzing fear is used by Satan to control our minds and keep us from doing the work of the Lord. I don't know if it was true or not, but my grandfather loved to tell the story about the time he was out quail hunting. He told how a hawk was flying over the area as he walked through a pine thicket. He saw a quail sitting on a branch in front of him. The quail was so scared of a hawk that it wouldn't move; it was paralyzed. My grandfather plucked the bird from the branch and put it in his bag. He took a few more steps, and there was another quail. One by one he plucked up the birds, and they didn't even attempt to fly. True or not, this story reminds us how Satan, through fear, can cause us to freeze up rather than to do God's will. He keeps us in our comfort zones. Instead of witnessing, we are afraid. Instead of following the Lord in the ministry, maybe as a missionary in a foreign land, a pastor, or teacher, whatever God would have us do, we freeze. Paul tells Timothy, "For God hath not given us the spirit of fear; but of power, and of love, and of a sound mind" (2 Tim. 1:7).

Break out of that comfort zone that holds you captive. God is love. "There is no fear in love; but perfect love casteth out fear: because fear hath torment. He that feareth is not made perfect in love" (1 John 4:18). Doing things by the power of the Holy Spirit and for the love of our God with a sound mind makes us relentless in the task at hand. He gives us the strength to not give up, thereby winning the battle against the power of the air.

Satan's next tool of distraction is very powerful especially in our day. You don't have to look too hard to see that Satan is in the entertainment business. He controls Hollywood and the music industry. People there flaunt themselves as an adulterous and perverted generation, influencing our children in a godless way and bringing a nation so far from God that we may be to a point of no return. As parents, we put our children in front of the television and give our children music so that they will be entertained while we are entertained since we don't make time to entertain them ourselves.

We are a generation that must be entertained at all times. Quiet time with the Lord is unheard of, and resting on Sunday is foolishness to many. There was a time in this nation when Sunday was considered the Lord's day. Families went to church to worship the Lord, sing praises of thanksgiving, and learn from the Word of God. Now it is a waste of time; and there is so much more to do, much like we read in Romans 1, which describes our nation. We saw that when the people are no longer thankful to God, they begin to worship the creature, or creation, rather than the creator. And they love their blessings rather than the blesser. Then we see the perverted lifestyles and the reprobate minds. Now Sunday is just another day. We shop, and we go to sporting events. We can watch television shows at any time on demand. Computers and games are always at our disposal. Satan has taken something that seems harmless and used it to distract and draw us away from the things of God. It reminds me of the children of Israel as they went into the Promised Land. The parents were to teach their children about how God had brought them out of the land of Egypt, but they failed. "And also all that generation were gathered unto their fathers: and there arose another generation after them, which knew not the LORD, nor yet the works which he had done for Israel" (Judges 2:10). They were distracted; and they followed after idols, fell into sin, and went from freedom into bondage. Isn't it funny how history repeats itself? We have raised a generation that can name all the hit movies and songs. They know the lyrics from beginning to end, and they know all the artists. They know sports heroes, scores, and teams; but if you ask them who Jesus Christ is and what He has done for them, they draw a blank. In fact, you might even hear crickets chirping as they mull over the question. We have been distracted from the things of God and have raised a generation that doesn't know the Lord.

Maddie and I continue to relax taking in the view. After several minutes, I hear the sound of a lonely crow off in the distance. The crow drops down and spots the hawk sitting on a tree limb finishing its meal. The crow calls to his friends, "Caw, caw, caw." One by one they come into sight, ten to twenty of them all at once, swooping down and flogging the hawk. They seem to be helping the smaller innocent game. As the hawk relentlessly preys on smaller, weaker animals, the crows appear to be the good guys. But crows, friends to no one, are self-centered, only looking out for themselves. They are scavengers. I have seen them flogging not only hawks but also gobblers and white-tailed bucks. Their desire is to be the greatest in the forest. They have been known to destroy nests and eat the eggs of smaller game birds. Years ago Rebecca and I were vacationing in Siesta Key, Florida. We decided to go for a walk along the white powdery sand. When we returned, there were two crows sitting on the back of our lounge chairs. They were looking out for the others while they went through our pool bags, scattering paper, pulling out and eating potato chips, and leaving nothing.

Unfortunately, in many of our churches, we have crows sitting on the church pews where they are scavenging and looking to destroy anyone they can. They are the gossipers and busybodies. They appear to be good because they are in church. They may be well-learned and faithful. They may know every song in the hymnbook, and they may speak out against Satan. Behind the scenes, Satan is controlling their lives. They are those who sow discord among the brethren, creating havoc in the local church. Because of these crows, I have seen young Christians leave and never look back, their spirits destroyed. The crows cause pastors and teachers grief and even depression. They produce a climate where the spirit of the Lord cannot work, a place where there is no happiness or joy. They are completely out to fulfil their own selfish desires. If that is not enough, they "caw" out into the community, where they spread the dirty laundry of the church into the community and make the church of no effect. No wonder Proverbs 6 says sowing discord among the brethren is one of the seven things that are abominations to the Lord. This discord is coupled with pride, which is exactly what caused Satan to fall from glory. It is unity, not division, that brings glory to God; love, not hatred; truth, not false witness; and a servant's heart, not pride. Living the life of a crow is very dangerous. Most people who do that have deceived themselves and don't even realize the damage they are causing. We must search our hearts diligently to make sure we don't open ourselves to such destruction. Be sober and vigilant; and know that our adversary, the devil, walks about seeking whom he may devour.

I noticed there was a silence throughout the forest when the hawk came on the scene. The squirrels were no longer barking, and the birds and their songs were silent. Only the faint sound of the katydids broke through until the hawk was completely out of sight. Before the hawk came on the scene, the symphony was in full swing. The squirrels were barking in the distance, and the songbirds were singing praises to God, things He designed them to do. As the hawk drew closer, some animals and birds began to shut down, and the symphony was no longer full. Without Satan, the world is full of praise to God, but through deception, he has led many astray and brought down that symphony of praise. The hawk draws closer causing more birds to shut down. Now it is no longer a symphony, just a few birds chirping. Satan through deception leads many astray, but through distractions, he leads many more and brings the level of praise even lower. The hawk is now in full view, and there is complete silence for fear of the hawk, knowing that any motion or sound would draw attention to the keen senses of the hawk. Only the weak sound of the katydids can now be heard in the distance.

Satan has desired to be like God. He desires the praise of man. While deceiving and distracting man, he will lead a great falling away from the truth of the gospel. He will set up his throne in the temple, where he will be worshipped through the Antichrist. The praise of God will be completely silent, out of fear. Those who are saved during this time called the tribulation, and who do not receive the mark of the beast, will be killed. There will be an eerie silence that will cover the earth, only the obnoxious sound of the crows will be heard as they gather together to seek, to destroy, and to praise Satan. While this is the scene on the earth, there will be a different scene in heaven. The Lord has promised to take his church out of this world through the rapture before the tribulation. This will be a time of praise that we have never seen before as we will see our Savior, the Lord Jesus Christ, the one who died on the cross to pay for our sins. We will see Him face-to-face. Will you be there praising God? Or will you be here on earth in that time of judgment?

After a short while, the hawk moves out of the area, and the sound of the crows fades into the distance. Peace and safety are there once again, and one by one the birds begin to sing. The woods seem full. After the tribulation is over, Jesus Christ will come and set up his kingdom here on earth. He will destroy those who fought against his people Israel, and He will judge the false prophet and the Antichrist. Satan will be bound and cast into the bottomless pit for one thousand years. During the one-thousand-year reign of Christ, there will be peace on earth, because Christ will be the king. This will be the millennial kingdom. There will be no more deception, no more distraction, and no more fear. There will be no more war or sickness, just peace and praise like this earth has never seen before. From the animals to the people, praise will ring out like no symphony we have ever heard.

As Satan seeks to destroy, we need help! We cannot go it alone. Satan is very powerful and not to be taken lightly. "For we wrestle not against flesh and blood, but against principalities, against powers, against the rulers of the darkness of this world, against spiritual wickedness in high places" (Eph. 6:12). This battle is not physical; this is spiritual warfare. We are fighting against spirits, not against other humans. We need the Lord Jesus Christ and His strength. If you have not trusted Jesus Christ to be your personal Savior, stop right now! Ask Him to be your Savior before it's too late. If He is not your Savior, you do not have His help or His strength. In fact, you are on Satan's side. Yes, you are one in Satan's army. If you have trusted the Lord Jesus Christ as your Savior, then you can read on to verses 13–18:

> Wherefore take unto you the whole armor of God, that ye may be able to withstand in the evil day, and having done all, to stand. Stand therefore, having your loins girt about with truth, and having on the breastplate of righteousness; And your feet shod with the preparation of the gospel of peace; Above all, taking the shield of faith, wherewith ye shall be able to quench all the fiery darts of the wicked. And take the helmet of salvation, and the sword of the Spirit, which is the word of God: Praying always with all prayer and supplication in the Spirit, and watching thereunto with all perseverance and supplication for all saints.

This battle cannot be fought with conventional weapons. Guns, tanks, and aircraft are worthless in this fight. Remember that we cannot go into it alone. We need the help of the Lord, and He is willing to give us that help, as He told Peter. "And the Lord said, Simon, Simon, behold, Satan hath desired to have you, that he may sift you as wheat" (Luke 22:31). Peter went into it alone on the night of Christ's betrayal. Peter denied the Lord three times and failed. Satan, who set out to destroy Peter's testimony, was successful. Satan seeks to sift us as wheat as well, but by allowing God to control our lives through the Holy Spirit, we can claim the promise of 1 John 4:4, "Ye are of God, little children, and have overcome them: because greater is he that is in you, than he that is in the world."

The question is, Who is controlling and influencing your life? Is it the Lord Jesus Christ through the Holy Spirit? Has Satan deceived you and blinded your eyes to the truth causing you to accept a counterfeit? Jesus said, "I am the way, the truth, and the life, no man cometh to the father but by me." Are you being distracted? Is your mind and life so full that you cannot focus on the Word of God? Maybe you are so caught up in the accomplishments for your own life that you are drawn away, and maybe these things are controlling you to the point they have become your lusts. James 1:13–15 tells us,

> Let no man say when he is tempted, I am tempted of God: for God cannot be tempted with evil, neither tempteth he any man: But every man is tempted, when he is drawn away of his own lust, and enticed. Then when lust hath conceived, it bringeth forth sin: and sin, when it is finished, bringeth forth death.

One sure way to failure is to be distracted. Distractions draw us away; and when we are drawn away, we lose our testimony, often believing the lies of Satan. Not only is our Christian life destroyed, but also quite possibly our physical life as well.

Have you allowed Satan to control your life with fear? The spirit of fear is not of God. Don't allow Satan to keep you in your comfort zone for fear of the unknown. If the Lord is moving in your heart, by all means go (whether in trusting Him for salvation or in some ministry He has for you). *Go!* Finally, we are told in James 4:7, "Submit yourselves therefore to God. Resist the devil, and he will flee from you." So be sober, be vigilant, seek the wisdom of God, and resist the devil; for he is as a roaring lion and he and his angels are the powers of the air, seeking whom they may devour.

THE HOOT OWL

After lunch Maddie and I head over the next ridge. I remember an old run-down house where two hollows run together and a stream crosses in what was formerly the front yard. A few grouse once hung around that area, so Maddie and I go in that direction. Eventually, we come to a large pine forest. The hollow is deep and dark. None of it is familiar. It has been several years since I was here. Seems like there should be a creek, but there is nothing here. We climb to the top of the next ridge and back down the next hollow, again up and down. I have gotten turned around, and I'm not exactly sure where I am.

The experience reminds me of a time many years ago when my cousins, Doc and Jabe, and I went to spend the week at our grandfather's cabin. Doc and I were about eight years old; Jabe was about five or six years old. We ran all through those woods, up and down old logging roads; we built forts; we played cowboys and Indians; and we probably had a fight or two. Our grandfather would give us such jobs as mowing the yard or cleaning up around the cabin while he made medical calls. Of course, those jobs would never get done, ringing true one of his favorite phrases, "One boy is a whole boy, two boys is a half a boy, and three boys is no boy at all." Then there was always one of my favorite sayings, "I'd like to buy you for what you are worth and sell you for what you think you are worth."

On Saturday afternoon, Granddad took us down to the river to do a little fishing. We didn't catch much of anything, only a little hornyhead. We cut it up and used it for bait, thinking we might catch a bigger fish. If my memory serves me correctly, I'm pretty sure we caught a turtle, which ended up breaking the line. Needless to say, if we were fishing for food, we would have gone to bed hungry that night. We fished until dark and headed back toward the cabin. We didn't realize that the fun was just about to begin.

The area had recently been logged, so there were several logging roads throughout the property. When we initially drove to the river, we came down a long hill, which was so steep we seemed to slide most of the way until we got to the river. Granddad decided to go back a different way. He took a few turns to make sure we were good and lost, well, at least we thought so. Every time we came to an intersection, Granddad would ask us, "Which way do you want to go?" Doc would yell out, "Let's go back up that steep hill!" We sat there for a few minutes, and Granddad contemplated, as if he did not know which way to go. He remarked, "Hmm, let's see what the hoot owl has to say." He climbed out of the old Bronco, and at the top of his lungs, he yelled, "Hoot! Hoot! Hoot owl, which way do we go?" He came back and told us the hoot owl said to go right. "What do you think? Should we follow the hoot owl or go back up the steep hill?" Jabe and I yelled out, "Follow the hoot owl!" Doc's mind would not be changed as he yelled, "Go back up that steep hill!" This rhetoric went on for several hours. Doc began to get pretty testy as he was determined to go back to the steep hill while Jabe and I continued to laugh knowing it was really getting under Doc's skin. You know, cousins are much like brothers, in that we like to find the weak point and push it until we cause trouble. Lost or not, it didn't really matter. After several hours of following the hoot owl, we could finally see the cabin in the distance. What a relief! As usual, Granddad had us going. He knew exactly where he was the whole time.

Many times we get turned around and sometimes downright lost in our lives. Wouldn't it be nice if we could just stop and call out to the hoot owl to give us guidance? Of course, there is no hoot owl, but thankfully, we have something better: our God through the Holy Spirit, the one who loves us, directs our paths, and we can call on Him at any time.

Years after that incident, I was hunting in the same area. I realized we had been all through those roads the day before. The only difference was that on the ride home it was dark. Things look a whole lot different when it is dark. For instance, when we are born in this world, we are born in darkness. "I am come a light into the world, that whosoever believeth on me should not abide in darkness" (John 12:46). Since we were born in darkness, Jesus Christ came to shine light so that we might see that our deeds are evil, repent of our sin, and come out of that darkness; but John 3:19 tells us that "men loved darkness rather than light." In Ephesians 6, we read that we wrestle against the rulers of the darkness of this world. Satan has blinded the minds of this world. By living in blindness, we cannot see, and if we cannot see, we are wandering in darkness and have lost our way.

I remember several years ago I was bow hunting from a tree stand, probably a quarter of a mile from my truck. I kept hearing something several yards below my stand. I had seen a good twelve-point buck in that area, so I waited hoping to get a shot. As time went on, it got dark, and I never saw the deer. So I climbed out of the stand to head back to the truck. Unfortunately, I forgot my flash-light. It was one of those nights that it was so dark I couldn't see my hand in front of my face. I kept running into trees, and I practically had to feel my way back.

Before trusting Jesus Christ as Savior, I was wandering around darkness: blind, not being able to discern which way to go, and feeling my way down a road of destruction. But as John 1:5 tells us, "The light shineth in darkness; and the darkness comprehended it not." In fact, the darkness flees. This light, Jesus Christ, the Light of the world, shines in our hearts as He did in mine. He showed me just how sinful I truly was and made me realize I needed salvation through Him. Once I was saved, that same light shines ahead and shows me the path of righteousness.

When we left the river and headed back to the cabin that night, we had a place to go. When I left my tree stand going to the truck, I had a place to go. Let me ask you, Where are you going? Where are you headed?

Many are satisfied just wandering aimlessly around in the dark. Satan has blinded their eyes and their minds, and that is the reason they love darkness. Unfortunately, this world is headed for destruction. Are you satisfied? There are many religions, all claiming a better place. If I asked you where you wanted to spend eternity, I'm sure you would say heaven, as all of us would. The question is, Do you know the way? Jesus talks about heaven.

> Let not your heart be troubled: ye believe in God, believe also in me. In my Father's house are many mansions: if it were not so, I would have told you. I go to prepare a place for you. And if I go and prepare a place for you, I will come again, and receive you unto myself; that where I am, there ye may be also. (John 14:1–3)

Jesus told his disciples not to be troubled because He was going to prepare a place for them. He didn't want to keep them in the dark. He was that Light, and the Light shows the way. Thomas was confused; he didn't understand how to get there even after being under the teaching of Jesus Christ all that time. Of course, we shouldn't look down on Thomas because there are many who have been raised in Christian families and have sat under some of the greatest preaching and still don't know the way. In verse 6, Jesus lets Thomas know He is "the way, the truth, and the life: no man cometh unto the Father, but by me."

The only way to get to heaven is through Jesus Christ our Lord. He is the Light that leads us out of darkness. Imagine a sailor out in the rough sea. A storm has caught him off guard. With the waves crashing all around and tossing the ship around like a small toy, the sailor can no longer tell which direction to turn. Finally, as he is about to give up, he sees the light from a lighthouse in the distance, and he sails toward the light to safety. Jesus is that lighthouse that shines even the darkest night, and He can bring one out of the most hopeless case. Jesus tells us in John 8:12, "I am the light of the world: he that followeth me shall not walk in darkness, but shall have the light of life."

I don't know about you, but I hate not being able to see where I am going. I'm thankful that Jesus Christ gives us that light so that we might see.

> Giving thanks unto the Father, which hath made us meet to be partakers of the inheritance

> of the saints in light: Who hath delivered us from the power of darkness, and hath translated us into the kingdom of his dear Son: In whom we have redemption through his blood, even the forgiveness of sins. (Col. 1:12–14)

Thank God, when we receive the Lord Jesus Christ as our Savior, we have an inheritance and a place in heaven and no longer have to walk in darkness. Because He is the Light and has destroyed the power of darkness, which no longer has control over us, we no longer have to walk in darkness. In fact, we are to reveal the Lord Jesus Christ in our lives in order that others might see the light of Christ in us and come to the light of Christ to be saved. We who believe are waiting on the blessed promise that "in my house are many mansions and if I go and prepare a place for you I will come again." When He receives us as His children, we become heirs and joint heirs with our Lord. It's all because of what Jesus did for us on Calvary's cross when He paid for our sins.

Jesus is the Light, flickering in the distance and calling for you to bring you from the tempestuous waves of destruction. Turn to the Light, open your eyes, and call upon the name of the Lord. It's only through Him. He is the way. When you see Him for who He is and for what He has done for you, believe on His name, and trust Him as your Savior, you can sing "Amazing Grace," the old hymn written by John Newton. "Amazing grace, how sweet the sound, that saved a wretch like me. I once was lost but now I'm found, was blind but now I see."

Once our eyes are opened, we can know the way, for we are no longer in darkness. God has brought us out of darkness and has saved us to the uttermost. Once we are saved by His grace, we are a new creature, and we set out to serve our new Father in heaven. Our new desire is to serve Him and to seek His will for our lives. We are now citizens of heaven. Our home is in heaven and no longer here on earth. We are pilgrims just passing through. We are a people wandering through a now unfamiliar world. Our desires are no longer of the world, and one day the Lord will take us home either through death or the rapture, whichever comes first.

The Pilgrims, searching for a better place to serve the Lord, left Europe to settle in Plymouth Rock and Jamestown. Though their citizenship was in Europe, they wandered through what is now the United States of America to seek the freedom to serve the Great God of Creation. Once we were in bondage to this world, citizens of this world, but now our citizenship is heaven, and we have the liberty to serve our great God until He calls us home.

"Thy word is a lamp unto my feet, and a light unto my path" (Ps. 119:105). Walking in the will of God can be confusing as God has given us the ability to make choices. We need the guidance of the Word of God, those very words that help us to not only make the right decisions but also let us know when we have made a mistake or gotten on the wrong path and become turned around. We must study the Word of God and prayerfully apply it to our own lives. How foolish it would be to carry a flashlight and never turn it on or shine it in the path. We must study the Word and let it guide us through the winding trails of life. By studying and incorporating these very words in our lives, we focus on the things of God, continually causing our whole life pattern to change for His glory.

God's Word is that lamp unto our feet and a light unto our path, but we need to study and learn His Word. He will give us the wisdom to stay on the path He has for us. We can easily become distracted, not taking the time to study and neglecting our prayer time. We can become so focused on other things we neglect our relationship with the Lord, which is most important. Before you realize it, the light has become dim, and you have wandered down a wrong trail away from the Lord.

When I was growing up raising sheep, I noticed many times a young lamb would be grazing with the flock with its head down and then it would look over and see a nice green patch of grass. The lamb would immediately go toward that grass and eat and would not pay any attention to the flock and its surroundings. While the flock moved in one direction, the young lamb moved in the other direction as it chased the desires of its heart and sought the luscious green grass. Before long, the lamb had gotten completely away from the fold and become lost.

In the old days, the shepherd would take his staff and hook the lamb around the neck and bring him back. If that lamb was prone to wander, the shepherd would be known to break the leg of the lamb so the lamb would no longer wander. Generally, after being nursed over the next several weeks, the lamb would learn to stay with the flock. I am reminded of the words in the old hymn "Come Thou Fount." The hymn writer talks about how we wander.

> O to grace how great a debtor daily I'm constrained to be! Let thy goodness like a fetter bind my wandering heart to thee: Prone to wander Lord I feel it, Prone to leave the God I love; here's my heart O take and seal it, seal it for thy courts above.[3]

I am oh so prone to wander, but thank God, He always brings me back. When Maddie was just a pup and trying to find her way, she decided it was more fun to chase deer. One Sunday afternoon we took a walk. Our walking trail was a good one hundred yards away from the road, but that wasn't far enough. Maddie jumped a deer on the side of the trail, and without hesitation, she was on its heels. As she headed straight for the busy highway, I called, but got no response. I looked for several minutes and probably ran a good mile looking for her. When I finally found her, I realized I would have to run her with an electronic collar to let her know when she has done wrong. She no longer runs deer; that collar saved her life.

Our God wants what is best for us. We are prone to wander and chase the desires of our hearts rather than seek the will of God. It is easy for us to get off on the trail of a deer when we are supposed to be hunting birds. We are His workmanship. He has a will and a purpose, and sometimes He has to shock us to get our attention. "Submit yourselves therefore to God. Resist the devil, and he will flee from you" (James 4:7). Submission means putting ourselves under the authority of God and His will for our lives.

---

3 "Come Thou Fount," in *Great Hymns of Faith*, page 17 verse 3.

When my daughter was in her teens, she was an equestrian. She rode horses in dressage and also in jumping events. Before she would begin to jump, she had to make sure the horse would submit to her authority over him. The horse often wanted to go his way and do his thing. In a technique called lunging, we would take a long rope and send the horse around in circles. While my daughter stood in the middle, the horse went around her. She commanded him to walk, trot, and then to canter. After a few minutes, she would make him change directions and do the same thing. In the beginning, the horse fought the rope. As we watched the horse's eyes, he would look away and try to turn his head away from his master. Every few steps my daughter would give a light jerk to bring his focus back to her. As long as he fought and wanted to go his way, he would continue to go around in circles.

Have you ever heard that when one is lost they always walk around in circles? When we are going our way rather than the Lord's way, we are going around in circles. After several laps in training, the horse quit fighting and began to turn his head toward his master to let her know that his focus was now on her. The horse was tired of fighting; he had humbled himself. Finally, after the command to whoa, the horse stopped; turned toward his master; and walked to her with his head lowered, licking his lips and chewing and letting her know that he was ready to do her will. He submitted. Are you still going in circles in your Christian life? Are you tired of fighting the Lord? Are you ready to submit to Him and His will for your life, the purpose that He has for you, or will you keep wandering?

It is Satan's desire to lead Christians astray. He influences our lives with distractions, causing us to turn from the truth of the Word of God. Paul warns us, "For the time will come when they will not endure sound doctrine; but after their own lusts shall they heap to themselves teachers, having itching ears; And they shall turn away their ears from the truth, and shall be turned unto fables" (2 Tim. 4:3–4). Paul tells Timothy that the time will come when people will not listen to the truth of the Bible but will instead go to hear preachers and teachers who make them feel good. Sin is no longer sin. It is not only acceptable but also embraced. These people teach that God is love and He would never judge anyone or send them to hell. They are deceiving and are being deceived. They have turned off the path of righteousness and are wandering on the path of fables and lies. Yes, we in America are in that time. We want pastors with whom we can drink a beer and someone who makes us feel good even when we are living in sin. For goodness sake, if you're about to walk off a cliff, wouldn't you want someone to tell you? That's why we need sound doctrine.

A friend of mine once told me that if the preacher hadn't offended him, he would have never trusted Jesus Christ as his Savior. Preaching today has become like a bad bottle of Coke. It has lost its fizz! Salvation is eternal, and Christians cannot be lost as far as salvation, but we can sure lose our way! Paul told Timothy, "Holding faith, and a good conscience; which some having put away concerning faith have made shipwreck" (1 Tim. 1:19). We hold the faith by sitting under preachers who preach sound doctrine and step on our toes, by studying the truth of the Word of God, by praying, having a close walk with our Lord, and allowing the Holy Spirit to direct our paths. We keep a good conscience by applying the Word to our lives and obeying. When we put away or ignore these things, we face shipwreck.

Paul knew about shipwreck as he experienced one on his way to Rome, but who can forget the tragic shipwreck of 1912 when the great luxury liner made its maiden voyage? The captain and crew set out to reach the States in record time. Well into the journey, other ships warned of icebergs in the area—we would call this truth. However, the captain ignored the call, the cry to humble himself and hear the truth. He believed the lie of his pride, and they all repeatedly ignored the warnings until it was too late. An iceberg ripped through the side of the great ship and sent it to the bottom of the Atlantic Ocean. The engineers were so sure of themselves that they didn't put enough lifeboats aboard the ship to save the passengers, should there have been a problem. While the ship was sinking, they used poor judgment and didn't load the few lifeboats they had with the capacity of people they should have been able to hold, causing further loss of life. It all began with self-sufficient pride, continued with the ignoring of the truth, and ended with shipwreck and destruction.

"Wherefore let him that thinketh he standeth take heed lest he fall" (1 Cor. 10:12).

When we, as Christians, drift or wander away from the Lord, live in our own power, and seek our own desires, look out for "shipwreck" is coming. When we head down this path, warnings will be ignored. One thing is for sure, every decision we make will affect someone else as we head for destruction. The engineers of the *Titanic*, the captain who could easily have chosen to slow down or take a more southern route, and those who loaded the lifeboats made decisions that affected so many more people than just themselves and led many to destruction.

When you drift away from the Lord, who are you taking with you? "But judge this rather, that no man put a stumbling block or an occasion to fall in his brother's way" (Rom. 14:13b). A stumbling block is something that would cause one to get tripped up and eventually fall. When we drift and are deceived by others and in turn influence one whom we should be helping, we are like the blind leading the blind. I have seen Christians who have grown up in Bible-believing churches and have been taught the truth get off on a false religion for whatever reason. Some Christians go so far as to claim that God does not exist. They live an atheist lifestyle, influencing others in the process and causing them to go astray.

I am reminded of the joke the farmers told as I was growing up. There was a young boy sitting in math class. He had trouble learning math, so his teacher asked him to solve a problem. There were four sheep in a fenced lot. One of the sheep got out. How many were left? The little boy studied a minute before answering, "Zero." The teacher replied, "You really don't know much about math." The little boy said, "You don't know much about sheep." When one sheep goes, they all go. They are influenced by each other. Isaiah said, "All we like sheep have gone astray."

Many of our children are indoctrinated by liberal colleges. They forget the things they were taught as children. Some of them go as far as to call the biblical teachings foolishness, and we wonder why our nation is in the shape that it is in. Others not only get off on the trail of false religion, but also get caught up in riotous living.

I am reminded of the great story of the prodigal son in Luke 15. To paraphrase, a man had two sons. The younger son decided he wanted his inheritance now. His father gave him his part, and this young man went out to spend it. The son was a big man now, especially in the eyes of those who wanted to take advantage of him. He lived it up—bar hopping, prostitutes, and maybe even a few drugs. This young man had everything at his disposal and a crowd to encourage him, but then he hit rock bottom and ran out of money. There was a famine in the land. Today we call that a recession. He had no money and no way of making money. This young man was in a situation in which he had no place to turn except to a man who gave him a job feeding the pigs. Jesus told this story to Jews, and in the minds of the Jews, the pig was an unclean, filthy animal. The young man was not only feeding the pigs but also eating with them. These actions showed the Jews that this young man was as low as he could go. A disgrace, he was looked down upon. Finally, the young man stopped and looked at himself. Have you ever done that before? Sometimes things are moving so fast we don't have time, but *stop*! Where are you? The young man looked at himself and remembered how well his father's servants were treated, and even they had bread enough to spare. He realized that his father's servants were far better off than he was, so he decided to swallow his pride and go back, not as a son but as a servant.

First, we see this young man realizes his condition. If you don't realize your condition, that you are headed down the wrong trail or that you are lost, you will continue to wander deeper and deeper until there is no turning back. Have you turned away from the will of God in your life? Do you no longer read the Word of God or spend time in prayer? Maybe you are much further along than that, to the point of rejecting God completely. Could it be alcohol, drugs, sex outside of marriage, or other things? You have to see yourself, and then you have to act.

> But be ye doers of the word, and not hearers only, deceiving your own selves. For if any be a hearer of the word, and not a doer, he is like unto a man beholding his natural face in a glass:

For he beholdeth himself, and goeth his way, and straightway forgetteth what manner of man he was. (James 1:22–24)

Each morning we climb out of bed and drag ourselves into the bathroom to get ready for another day. If you are a woman, you look at yourself, fix your hair, and maybe put on a little makeup. We call that painting the barn. Some people need two coats; others can do it in one. While women are painting the barn, we men have to mow the yard and rake the grass, unless you're like me. There are a few patches that are getting a little thin. Each year I feel like my hair is sliding off my head and down my back. Regardless, the things we see in the mirror we fix. We certainly wouldn't go out in public if we didn't. Had that young man not stopped and looked at himself, he would have never gone back home. He would have either starved to death or gotten some kind of disease as a result of eating with the hogs.

Oh, how sad it is when we walk away from the mirror without fixing those things that are out of place. This young man stopped, looked in the mirror, saw his mistake, and changed. He repented of his sin and turned back to his father. Is it time for you to turn back? Or are you going to keep running and wallowing in the mud with the pigs? When the young man swallowed his pride and made the long journey home, he recited through his mind over and over what he was going to say to his father, but his father had already heard of his return. As he topped the hill, his father saw him in the distance. He ran toward him with open arms and kissed him on the neck. The son said, "I have sinned against heaven, and in thy sight, and am no more worthy to be called thy son." However, the father told the servants to bring the best robe for him, put a ring on his hand and shoes on his feet, and kill the fatted calf. The father said, "Let us eat, and be merry: for this my son was dead, and is alive again; he was lost and is found."

The father rejoiced as his son returned home. There was a celebration. How much more is the rejoicing in heaven when one repents and comes back to the Lord! I can only imagine the pain of the father who had raised his children and taught them the things of God, yet that child went astray. I believe that man spent a lot of time on his knees. He was closer to God than ever before. A few years ago I wrote these words while praying for my children:

> Train up a child in the way he should go, was that proverb told, and he will not depart from it whenever he grows old, but this old world has promised you happiness and fame, but it's delivered broken hearts, sorrow and shame, and it's my earnest prayer for you that God will change your heart and bring you to your knees, where I'll be waiting, down on my knees praying, cause I'm already there.

That father loved his son dearly. Our Father in heaven knows what is best for you and me. He loves us enough to save us. Does He not love us enough to forgive us when we repent of our sins?

Finding God's will for your life gives you peace. Many times we, as servants of the Lord, are living for Him; then out of the blue, without warning, misfortune or tragedy strikes. All of us at some time will face a life-changing experience or tragedy in our lives. As a Christian, maybe you don't think this type of thing is possible, but God never promised that life would be a bed of roses. Yes, He said, "My yoke is easy, and my burden is light," but He is talking about salvation. In salvation, we have the Holy Spirit dwelling within us and giving us the strength and peace to endure these situations. Through our Lord, we can have peace within no matter the chaos without. During this time, you are in a place or position where you have never been. You are walking an unfamiliar road that you have never traveled. You may even feel lost. It could be so many things: a diagnosis, a tragic loss, financial problems, a rebellious child. Whatever it is, if you could get off this road, you would certainly never go back. You would not wish this pain and anguish, this uncertainty, on your worst enemy. You don't know which way to turn, and you are in desperate need of help. I wrote these words several years ago:

> The storm clouds are rolling, the thunder sounds near, uncertainty lingers, my heart's full

of fear, at the end of the tunnel I can't see the light, but my Savior reminds me, walk by faith and not sight.

These are the dark times in our lives. If we could only see the path, yet it seems we wander aimlessly in darkness. Just like calling on the hoot owl, we can call on our Lord. We have to put our faith in Him and walk by faith and not sight.

I am reminded of the psalm of the great shepherd.

> The LORD is my shepherd; I shall not want. He maketh me to lie down in green pastures: he leadeth me beside the still waters. He restoreth my soul: He leadeth me in the paths of righteousness for his name's sake. Yea, though I walk through the valley of the shadow of death, I will fear no evil: For thou art with me; Thy rod and thy staff they comfort me. Thou preparest a table before me in the presence of mine enemies: Thou anointest my head with oil; my cup runneth over. Surely goodness and mercy shall follow me all the days of my life: and I will dwell in the house of the LORD forever. (Ps. 23)

The Lord is our shepherd, and He will be with us all the way. Notice in the psalm, he maketh, he leadeth, and he restoreth, making our cup to run over. Surely because our Savior leads us all the way, goodness and mercy shall follow us all the days of our lives. In the famous poem "Footprints in the Sand," there were two sets of prints through the easy times, but throughout the hard times, there was only one set of prints. The writer turns to the Lord and asks, "Where were you through the hard times? I saw your prints when things were going well, but when I really needed you, they disappeared." The Lord answered, "Those were the times I carried you."

If I could only tell you how much God loves you and how much He cares for you even in the little things of life! He is our shepherd, and the shepherd cares for the sheep. Trust in the Lord. He'll see you through. Cast your cares upon Him, for He careth for you.

Maddie and I continue walking down a long hollow. I hear the trickle of a small stream. Things begin to look a little more familiar. I see the old white oak trees that once majestically stood around the yard and brought shade to the old house. Much of the house has now fallen down. The stone chimney is a pile of rubble. Briars and grapevines have taken over the house as well as a couple of apple trees out back. I cannot help but to think what it must have been like here several years ago. I can imagine the laughter of many children, maybe ten or more, as they played in the creek below. The mom and dad probably didn't have two pennies to rub together, but they worked hard to keep everything going. The children all had jobs to do, and they helped each other. The chickens produced eggs, and the old milk cow produced milk. The family was self-sufficient as they hunted for meat, and even though they didn't have much materially, they loved each other. They were thankful for what they had. The Bible was taught on a daily basis. There was prayer before each meal, and the family was probably spiritually wealthier than any family in our nation today.

As I look at this run-down house, I think of a nation that has lost its way. When the family is gone and the home is broken down, the churches then begin to fall apart. Children no longer play in the churchyard; they have no desire. The older generation will only be around a few more years, and then those buildings will also be empty and falling down. The communities will begin to fall; and finally, the nation, a nation that was founded on the principles of the Word of God, will follow.

Probably the greatest missionary nation in history has become a mission field, because our children do not know the Lord and what He has done for us. We have taken a wrong trail. We have gotten turned around and don't know which way to go, but it's not too late.

> If my people, which are called by my name,
> shall humble themselves, and pray, and seek my
> face, and turn from their wicked ways; then I will
> hear from heaven, and forgive their sin, and will
> heal their land. (2 Chron. 7:14)

A nation is healed one person at a time. Are you aimlessly wandering through life without a purpose, not knowing which way to turn or where you are headed? Call on the Lord. Maybe you once had peace, but now uncertainty reigns in your life as you have gotten off the trail. You could be like the prodigal son, and you're at a crossroads. Stop! Call on the Lord. Take the words of Paul to heart and claim them. "For whosoever shall call upon the name of the Lord shall be saved" (Rom. 10:13).

It is a relief to finally be on familiar ground and such a comfort and joy to know where I am. Imagine the joy and comfort you can know by turning or returning to the Savior, no longer living in uncertainty and aimlessly wandering with no purpose, but having joy and being safe in the will of God.

MADDIE'S BROKEN LEG

So far Maddie and I have had a pretty good day. We haven't killed any grouse, but we have flushed a few. It is getting later in the afternoon, and Maddie is still going strong. She is giving me all she's got. As she pushes on, I can see she is getting a little tired. When Maddie gets tired, she favors her right rear leg. In fact, as she runs down the hill, she actually has a tendency to carry it, making sure to protect it from harm.

We brought Maddie home in late March or early April. She was a gift from my cousin Doc, with whom I have hunted most of my life. The deal was to take her for breeding, so we could keep this line going. Doc would also get the pick of the litter when she had puppies. She came to us during a difficult time in our family and brought us a lot of joy. We already had two Weimaraners, but Maddie came in and stole the show. She would lay between the two big dogs and force them off the bed, and when she got wound up, she would jump all over them. I'm sure they would have eaten her if they could, as she chewed on their big floppy ears.

One warm spring day I took the dogs out for a walk. At three months old, Maddie was really strutting her stuff as she pranced around hunting for birds. The Weimaraners had gotten a little ahead of us, and I changed direction to go down a different trail. I called the dogs, and they came running. Unfortunately, Lilly, being a good fifty pounds, didn't see Maddie as she came around the corner and ran right over her. That poor girl yelped at the top of her lungs. I tried to comfort her and hoped it was only a bruise, but Maddie's leg was broken. Maddie required a few hours of surgery and several months of checkups, and I have come to the conclusion there is no such thing as a free hunting dog. We nursed Maddie back, and she continues to be a good hunting dog. Although she carries that leg, she doesn't allow it to slow her down.

Many times as Christians we have things in our past that we allow to get us down and keep us down. Maybe those things are sins that we committed either before or after we were saved. Some people don't come to Jesus Christ because of past sins they have committed. They think it would be impossible for God to save them from the evil they have done. Yes, there are people who have committed heinous crimes and destroyed the lives of others and might even be sitting on death row. You think to yourself, there is no way someone like that can be saved. I would like to tell you today that the past is in the past. Today is the day of salvation! All have sinned against the Holy God. He sent His only son to die for *all* the sins of the world. All means all, all of the time, and that's all that all means.

If you are still alive and breathing, you can accept the gift of God, the Lord Jesus Christ, for salvation and the forgiveness of sins. As He hung on the cross, He died for every sin that ever was committed and every sin that ever will be committed. There is no sin so great that His sacrifice didn't satisfy the payment. He paid the price in full. Romans 6:23 says, "The wages of sin is death." The word *wages* means payment or cost. I work in the car business. If you come to me to buy a car and I price a car for $5,000, the price is $5,000, no more, no less. The price is dollars. I don't want chickens, cows, pesos, or euros. There are many people trying to pay for their sins through works and rituals, but that is not the cost of sin. The cost of sin is death! Without the shedding of blood, there is *no remission*! Our Lord Jesus Christ, the perfect Lamb of God, shed His blood and died the death on the cross to pay the price for *all* sin. When you believe on the Lord Jesus Christ, ask Him to be your Savior and forgive you for your sins and repent, which means to turn away. Your sins are then forgiven and forgotten. David pens it perfectly: "As far as the east is from the west, so far hath he removed our transgressions from us" (Ps. 103:12). As far as the east is from the west, He has removed our sins from us, and He has buried them in the deepest sea. I like the way Pastor James Cockram adds, "And then he put a sign out that says *no fishing*," as our sins are forgiven and forgotten.

I saw a sign on a church the other day: "A sinner has a past, but a saint has a future." If you reject the gift of God and His payment for your sins, you will be held accountable for every sin that you have committed. In other words, your past will be remembered. Jesus said in John 3:18,

> He that believeth on him is not condemned:
> but he that believeth not is condemned already,
> because he hath not believed in the name of the
> only begotten Son of God.

Being condemned, you will stand before that great white throne of judgment. Each sin will be brought up and will be judged accordingly. Mercy and grace will then be gone. The righteous judge will pass down the sentence of death and eternal punishment; and you will be cast into the lake of fire, which will burn forever and ever and where there will be weeping, wailing, and gnashing of teeth. Imagine the pain and suffering.

While the unbelievers are suffering for eternity, we who believe will enter into the presence of a holy and perfect God and live forever. Oh, the wages of sin are death and hell, but the gift of God is eternal life through Jesus Christ our Lord. Those who reject Christ and His salvation will stand at that judgment, and I believe they will remember their loved ones who pled with them to accept the gift of God. They might recall reading this book and wish they had received Him as Savior. Wouldn't you rather have forgiveness? Receiving the gift of God is receiving forgiveness of sin. Our past is now forgotten, and we only have a future, the future of abundant and eternal life in Christ. Thanks be to God for His unspeakable gift! No matter what you have done in your life, our Almighty God is greater, His grace is greater, and His love is greater than all of our sins.

One of my favorite passages in the Bible is Romans 5:6–8.

> For when we were yet without strength, in
> due time Christ died for the ungodly. For scarcely
> for a righteous man will one die: yet peradven-

ture for a good man some would even dare to
die. But God commendeth his love toward us,
in that, while we were yet sinners, Christ died
for us.

Verse 6 really stands out: "It is rare that, for a good man one
would die." This reminds me of one of our bravest. On September
29, 2006, Michael Monsoor of the Delta Platoon was patrolling in
Ramadi. While on patrol, a grenade was thrown by an insurgent
onto the roof top, endangering Michael and his fellow soldiers. He,
without hesitation, threw himself onto the grenade, absorbing the
blast and sacrificing his own life while saving his comrades. Michael
Monsoor, a true American hero, died for his own and the good men;
but Jesus Christ willingly died on the cross of Calvary while we were
His enemies, not friends and not good men (for there is none good)
so we would be justified and declared righteous through faith in
Christ Jesus and His precious blood.

How could God love us so much? I can't explain it, but I can
believe. I did receive the gift of salvation, and you can too. Your past
is in the past. Your sins can be blotted out, and your slate can be
wiped clean. "Therefore if any man be in Christ, he is a new creature:
old things are passed away; behold, all things are become new" (2
Cor. 5:17). If you will only believe, you will be saved.

That if thou shalt confess with thy mouth
the Lord Jesus, and shalt believe in thine heart
that God hath raised him from the dead, thou
shalt be saved. For with the heart man believeth
unto righteousness; and with the mouth confession is made unto salvation. (Rom. 10:9–10)

As a Christian, you have made the choice to trust Jesus Christ
and have been forgiven for all of your past sins. As you go through
your daily walk of life, you might have a burden of something that
you have done in the past. This burden has been causing you guilt. It
could have been something you did before salvation or maybe after

you were already saved. First, have you confessed it to the Lord and asked for forgiveness? Second, have you repented of that sin? If the sin was committed against someone else, then you need to go to that one and get it straight with them as well. Once these things are done, there is nothing else we can do; but know that Satan, the great accuser, will not forget even though our Lord has forgiven and forgotten. Satan will also constantly remind you of that sin. He will cause it to be a burden to you, making you feel inadequate and keeping you from doing the work of the Lord. If Maddie decided she could no longer run and hunt because her leg was broken in the past, she wouldn't be able to serve the purpose for which she was bred. In fact, she would be a complete waste. Well, maybe not. She is a pretty good ol' girl, but you get the point. In order for us to be the servant God would have us to be, we must put the past in the past, trust that He will forgive us, and move on.

We do need to understand that although God does forgive us of our sins, there are consequences. Maddie's leg was broken. Even though it is healed now and in the past, the consequence of that break is that she carries it in a different way. Think of someone who has abused alcohol most of his life to the point he has damaged his liver. If this one trusts Jesus Christ as Savior, his sins are forgiven. If he has allowed Christ to change his life and has completely turned from the alcohol, he has made a lifestyle change, and the past is in the past. Unfortunately, the consequence of that sin may be a destroyed liver. Sin has its consequences, but God has forgiveness, which is far greater. We can take our sins to Him and leave them at the cross.

As I think on this issue that we all face in our lives, I cannot help but think of the apostle Paul. Paul was probably one of the greatest missionaries to ever live. The Lord used Paul to bring His name before kings and throughout the Gentile nations, but Paul had a wicked past. He was a Pharisee, a religious leader of his day. He was educated and mentored under the great high priest Gamaliel and was well-versed in the Old Testament scriptures. Paul was privileged with dual citizenship. He was a full-blooded Jew and a Roman citizen, giving him more rights than many other Jews. He describes himself in Philippians 3:4–6:

> Though I might also have confidence in the flesh. If any other man thinketh that he hath whereof he might trust in the flesh, I more: Circumcised the eighth day, of the stock of Israel, of the tribe of Benjamin, an Hebrew of the Hebrews; as touching the law, a Pharisee; Concerning zeal, persecuting the church; touching the righteousness which is in the law, blameless.

Paul had an honorable pedigree; he was a Pharisee of Pharisees. He was a zealous and a tenacious man. A go-getter, we might say. Many people thought highly of Paul because in their eyes he was a righteous man, blameless. That observation could not have been further from the truth. Paul was on the wrong road. As a self-righteous man, he set out to destroy the church and the name of Christ. Originally, he went by the name Saul in the book of Acts. Saul of Tarsus was his Hebrew name. In Acts 13:9, he was later referred to as Paul, his Roman or Greek name.

Saul is first mentioned at the death of Stephen in Acts 7:58, "And cast him out of the city, and stoned him: and the witnesses laid down their clothes at a young man's feet, whose name was Saul." He was present and took part at the stoning of Stephen, one of the great men of faith. More light is shed on him in Acts 8:1, 3.

> And Saul was consenting to his death. And at that time there was a great persecution against the church which was at Jerusalem; and they were all scattered abroad throughout the regions of Judea and Samaria, except the apostles... As for Saul, he made havock of the church, entering into every house, and haling men and women committed them to prison.

Here's a man who had a part in murder and the false accusation and imprisonment of innocent men and women. He sought to snuff out the name of Christ by destroying everyone associated with that name, but God has a way of changing hearts.

In Acts 9:1–2, he begins his final mission of living for religion and the flesh, the last trip down the road of destruction.

> And Saul, yet breathing out threatenings and slaughter against the disciples of the Lord, went unto the high priest, And desired of him letters to Damascus to the synagogues, that if he found any of this way, whether they were men or women, he might bring them bound unto Jerusalem.

Saul was seeking anyone who proclaimed Jesus Christ as Savior. As he set out to destroy more Christians, he met Jesus on that old road to Damascus, and his life was changed forever.

Have you met Jesus? He will change your life too. Paul saw that great light and was blinded. He lay there as Jesus asked him, "Why do you persecute me?" Saul never forgot those words as he was led to Damascus. He had time to meditate on his past. He saw his sin and repented. From that time forward he truly served the Lord the rest of his days. Saul's sins were forgiven. He was ready to serve the Lord, but to others he still had a past. Meanwhile, the Lord spoke to a man named Ananias in a vision.

> And there was a certain disciple at Damascus, named Ananias; and to him said the Lord in a vision, Ananias. And he said, Behold, I am here, Lord. And the Lord said unto him, Arise, and go into the street which is called Straight, and enquire in the house of Judas for one called Saul, of Tarsus: for, behold, he prayeth, And hath seen in a vision a man named Ananias coming in, and putting his hand on him, that he might receive

his sight. Then Ananias answered, Lord, I have heard by many of this man, how much evil he hath done to thy saints at Jerusalem: And here he hath authority from the chief priests to bind all that call on thy name. But the Lord said unto him, Go thy way: for he is a chosen vessel unto me, to bear my name before the Gentiles, and kings, and the children of Israel: For I will shew him how great things he must suffer for my name's sake. (Acts 9:10–16)

Knowing that Saul had the power to commit him to prison, Ananias had to trust God and put the past in the past. Saul had an awful past, but the Lord had already changed his heart. I like verse 20 in this passage: "And straightway he preached Christ in the synagogues, that he is the Son of God." A few days earlier, Saul was out to destroy anyone who named the name of Christ, and now without delay, he puts it in the past and preaches Christ Himself. He is no longer a servant to Satan but rather a proclaimer of the good news of the gospel and a chosen vessel to bring the good news to the Gentiles, kings, and the nation of Israel. He is a soldier of Christ.

Paul had a past, but he had to put his past in the past. Are you allowing your past to hold you back? Paul wrote in Philippians 3:12–14,

Not as though I had already attained, either were already perfect: but I follow after, if that I may apprehend that for which also I am apprehended of Christ Jesus. Brethren, I count not myself to have apprehended: but this one thing I do, forgetting those things which are behind, and reaching forth unto those things which are before, I press toward the mark for the prize of the high calling of God in Christ Jesus.

Paul had a goal to do the will of God. He didn't live as though he had already accomplished that goal. He not only put his successes behind him but also his sinful past, which had to be left behind in order to move forward with the things of God. Yes, Paul had a past but God gave him a future.

The sinful, dark times in our lives are the valleys in our lives; and the high points, in which we are thankful and proud, are the mountains. But time goes on. Repent of the sin and ask for forgiveness. Rejoice in the good times and be thankful. But put the past in the past, move on, and reach for the things that are before. Yes, it would be great if we could go back and make changes to the past. I don't know about you, but I would waste the rest of my life cleaning up the mistakes that I have made in the past, rather than learning from my mistakes and moving forward. I think about the great athletes in our day. Many athletes have great physical ability to perform, but they lack the mental capacity to become truly successful. A successful athlete must have a short memory. There will be times they make mistakes, but the great ones put the mistakes behind them and move on. For instance, a quarterback throws an interception in the first quarter of a game, and the opponent runs it back for a touchdown. Is the game over? Does he just quit, go and sit on the sideline, and cry about it? Does he leave the stadium and go do something else? Of course not! He's the leader, and he has to put it behind him. It's in the past. In this case, the whole team is counting on the quarterback to pick himself up, acknowledge his mistake, learn from it, and go and finish strong. The Lord gives Christians power through the Holy Spirit to overcome our sins, and He is counting on us to move forward and do His work for His glory. I'll also bet there are others who are watching you. How you handle situations will influence how they move forward in their lives. Many times we are examples. We don't even realize people are watching.

We must understand that we will fall short and make mistakes. We must put those mistakes behind us, but we also need to learn from each mistake. My granddad once said, "It's okay to make a mistake, just don't make the same one twice." In watching Maddie run, I can see she has learned that leg can be hurt. She is going to protect that leg making sure it doesn't happen again. As Christians, we need to examine ourselves regularly so that we may learn from our sins and our accomplishments, not dwelling on them but putting them in the past. We need to reach forward, not behind, and use these experiences to grow and glorify God. Putting things in the past is always easier said than done. While we long to do so, Satan wants to use our past to keep us from serving the Lord. We in the flesh are weak. Once again, we need the help of our Lord. Go to God in prayer. He has given us that great privilege to go to Him at any time. He has promised us the Holy Spirit, that one called alongside to help, which indwells each of His children. Jesus said, "Whatsoever ye ask in my name, that will I do." It is certainly not God's will for His children to go around worrying about the past. What kind of testimony do we have when we ask for forgiveness yet don't have enough faith to believe that He can forgive us? Jesus Christ our Lord died on a cross to pay for all of our sins; therefore, we must confess our sins to Christ and by faith leave those sins at the cross!

As Christians, it is a great feeling to know our sins are forgiven and put in the past. Looking forward, we will sin sometimes, and we will commit the same sin more than once, but thankfully, we have a promise. "If we confess our sins, he is faithful and just to forgive us our sins, and to cleanse us from all unrighteousness" (1 John 1:9). A child who makes a mistake goes to his father and says, "I'm sorry. Please forgive me." We can go to our Father in heaven, and He will forgive our sins. We spend a lot of time concerned that our Lord has forgiven us. We sin against God and then fall on our knees as the guilt seems to consume our hearts. We say, "Oh Lord, please forgive me for my actions," yet are we willing to forgive others when they offend us? Paul tells us, "And be ye kind one to another, tenderhearted, forgiving one another, even as God for Christ's sake hath forgiven you" (Eph. 4:32). God forgave you for your sins. Are you willing to forgive others who have sinned against you? No matter how hard it may be to forgive, no matter how wrong the wrong was, or how devastating, we must forgive as Christ has forgiven us. That means putting it is in the past as He has put our sins in the past. Peter came to Jesus with a question in Matthew 18:21. "Then came

Peter to him, and said, Lord, how oft shall my brother sin against me, and I forgive him? Till seven times?" In those days the rabbis taught that one was to forgive three times. Peter feeling generous asked if he ought to forgive seven times, but Jesus quickly pointed out he needed to forgive far more than that. "Jesus saith unto him, I say not unto thee, Until seven times: but, Until seventy times seven." That statement meant not just 490 times. There are to be no limits on how many times we forgive someone.

Many Christians walking around us are forgiven, yet they cannot forgive. They hold grudges and will not let anything go, even when the one who wronged them apologizes and asks for forgiveness. As Jesus was teaching his disciples about forgiveness, he used a parable to make his point. A parable is an earthly story with a heavenly truth or meaning. The story comes from Matthew 18:23–35.

> Therefore is the kingdom of heaven likened unto a certain king, which would take account of his servants. And when he had begun to reckon, one was brought unto him, which owed him ten thousand talents. But forasmuch as he had not to pay, his lord commanded him to be sold, and his wife, and children, and all that he had, and payment to be made. The servant therefore fell down, and worshipped him, saying, Lord, have patience with me, and I will pay thee all. Then the lord of that servant was moved with compassion, and loosed him, and forgave him the debt. But the same servant went out, and found one of his fellowservants, which owed him an hundred pence: and he laid hands on him, and took him by the throat, saying, Pay me that thou owest. And his fellowservant fell down at his feet, and besought him, saying, Have patience with me, and I will pay thee all. And he would not: but went and cast him into prison, till he should pay the debt. So when his fellowservants saw what

was done, they were very sorry, and came and told unto their lord all that was done. Then his lord, after that he had called him, said unto him, O thou wicked servant, I forgave thee all that debt, because thou desiredst me: Shouldest not thou also have had compassion on thy fellows-ervant, even as I had pity on thee? And his lord was wroth, and delivered him to the tormentors, till he should pay all that was due unto him. So likewise shall my heavenly Father do also unto you, if ye from your hearts forgive not everyone his brother their trespasses.

Here the Lord shows us just how hypocritical we can be to others as we are forgiven but are not willing to forgive.

People are people. None of us are perfect. We will offend others, and there will be times when one will not apologize. We are offended and angry about what was said or done. Paul tells us in Ephesians 4:26–27, "Be ye angry, and sin not: Let not the sun go down on your wrath: Neither give place to the devil." It is not a sin to be angry. Our Lord was angered as he walked into His Father's house (the temple) and they had made it a den of thieves, like a regular flea market. The problem is we need to deal with anger and not dwell on it. When anger is allowed to fester, it becomes like an infection. It soon becomes something far worse, and the believer is now living in sin. Nine times out of ten, you hold a grudge and hang on to that bitterness toward someone else and they have absolutely no idea you are even angry. While you are stressing and all in a knot, guess what? It's not hurting them at all. You need to go to that one in love, of course, not in hatred, and let them know they are doing something that offends you. They may not even realize what they are doing. They may be so ashamed when you go to them that they apologize and make it right. You stressed over nothing. Here in America, we have become so thin-skinned that everything offends us. If you are offended regularly, you probably need to check yourself. You may need to just toughen up.

Unfortunately, as time goes on, persecution seems to be inevitable. Let's be honest, our nation is turning completely away from our Christian roots, and as Christians stand for the things of God, our message will not be popular with many people in society. Over the past few years, we have seen lawsuits against Christians because they didn't support certain unbiblical marriages. Christians have and will continue to face threats from every level because many people are offended by the stances taken by Christians. When taking biblical stances, we must be firm and not waver, and we cannot apologize, because as Peter and the apostles proclaimed in Acts 5:29, "We ought to obey God rather than men." Yes, God has the final say. His ways are right.

When early Christians were persecuted, they stood to the death and many times willingly gave their lives for the one who gave His life for them. Even though we will suffer at the hand of angry people, we must still be willing to forgive. I am reminded of one of my favorite Bible characters, Stephen. Just after the first mention of Saul, Dr. Luke tells us of the death of Stephen. Stephen stood before the people and preached the Word of God, which was not received well at all. In rage, the people dragged Stephen out of the city. They gnashed on him with their teeth, literally bit him, and stoned him to death. The rocks came flying and were continually hitting him when in excruciating pain, Stephen called out to God, "Forgive them for they know not what they do." Stephen stood firm, and he spoke the truth. Often the truth hurts. In this case, it cut them to the heart, and while they set out to kill Stephen, he forgave them and prayed that God would forgive them too. This is our example. Stephen referenced the very words of our Savior, Jesus Christ our Lord, who was beaten and nailed to the cross to pay for our sins. As He hung on the cross, the mob mocked Him, laughed at Him to scorn, and cried out, "You saved others. Save yourself." But just before our Lord gave up the ghost, He cried with a loud voice, "Forgive them for they know not what they do." Jesus Christ took all of our sins, paid for them in full, and then forgave us for them. He put them all in the past.

Maddie continues to run up and down the side of the mountain, and as she carries her leg, it seems a little awkward. The bone was once broken, but it is now healed. The bone, which grew back together, is probably stronger than it was before. The point is, all this is in the past. Maddie moves as if she knows it can happen again, but it doesn't slow her down.

Are you living in the past? Are you concerned over past sins, afraid you will be held accountable? Have you believed on the Lord Jesus Christ and trusted Him as your Savior? Have you been saved and committed a sin that you think there is no way the Lord could forgive you? He paid for all sins and will forgive all sins if we ask Him to do so. Maybe you are holding a grudge against someone that has wronged you in the past? Forgive as Christ forgave. Whether you have spent your past on the peaks or in the valleys, these things are in the past. God cannot use one who keeps looking back. Jesus says in Luke 9:62, "No man, having put his hand to the plough, and looking back, is fit for the kingdom of God." Put the past in the past and reach forward as you are glorifying God and looking toward that blessed day when we will see Him face-to-face.

ROUGH TERRAIN

Maddie and I top over a knoll and move into a small grassy field. It sure feels good after walking several miles through the mountains. It seems I've been on an incline all day. My ankles are sore, and my legs are tired. The grass is still green and soft under my feet. Oh, it's so pleasant to walk on this terrain after walking over hard rock all day. The field is only a little over an acre, and on the other side, there is a narrow grassy road that leads around to the next ridge. On either side of the road, the timber has grown tall, and there is no cover or food for the grouse. Although the trail feels so good to my feet, I know that if I'm going to find any more birds, I need to change course.

Ruffed grouse thrive in thick cover, green briars, grapevines, and rough terrain to protect them from predators and provide food. If I'm going to be successful, I will have to go to them. I walk on until I come to the next deep hollow, full of grapevines and briars. Maddie must have caught the scent of a grouse. Her tail begins to wag a little faster in excitement. Knowing there is probably a grouse nearby, she heads down into the deep ravine. I follow close behind her. My first step is down a steep incline. I stumble over a few large rocks. The ground seems to move under my feet. I fall forward and bang up my knee as I fall to the ground. It is almost like a fairy tale, the grapevines wrapping around my legs as I pull myself up to continue on. The green briars reach out and take hold of my shirt, and at that moment the branch from a wild cherry tree snaps around and hits me in the face. Ouch! That's going to leave a mark. I put my head down, and with the protection of my Australian outback hat, I keep moving down the slope.

In the Christian life, the easy way is not always the best way. You can walk on the smooth road, and it feels good. You will probably never have any challenges or rough terrain to face. If you set out to truly serve and live a Christ-centered, sacrificial life, standing for the Lord, look out, for the opposition is coming! As you can see, I'm not a member of the health, wealth, and prosperity movement. I think it is deceitful; and it can easily destroy young Christians, especially ones who have been taught if they give their hearts to Christ and then serve the Lord with all their beings, somehow everything is going to be wonderful—a bed of roses, success, prosperity. You get my drift, right?

When you serve the Lord, you are going against the grain, against the world. Jesus tells us in Matthew 6:24, "No man can serve two masters: for either he will hate the one, and love the other; or else he will hold to the one, and despise the other. Ye cannot serve God and mammon." The word *mammon* is translated "money." It comes from the Aramaic word for "wealth" or "property," and it can also be used as "treasure," things of the world.

John writes in 1 John 2:15, "Love not the world, neither the things that are in the world. If any man love the world, the love of the Father is not in him." Understand that being wealthy and prosperous does not mean that you are serving the Lord. Neither does being poor make you a saint. The health, wealth, and prosperity movement has many people believing if they have much gain and success, they are somehow better Christians than someone who is barely getting by. It also gives the idea if they trust Jesus Christ as Savior, they will achieve great physical and material gain. God blesses some with wealth and prosperity. At the same time, He may bless others with persecution, poor health, or just enough to get by. Remember Jesus said, "The last shall be first, and the first shall be last." Did you ever think when you have hit the bottom and you have nowhere else to turn, when every avenue you have tried seems to fail, you have to look up and say, "Okay, Lord, I give it all to you." At that point you are closer to God than ever before, and that's a greater blessing than being the wealthiest man on earth.

Paul is believed to have written the Epistle to the Philippians from a prison cell. Some people believe it was located in Rome while others thought it was in Caesarea. Either way he was in a trying place. This man had devoted his life to serve the Lord, and he found the words to write in Philippians 4:11, "Not that I speak in respect of want: for I have learned, in whatsoever state I am, therewith to be content." Paul had come to the conclusion that no matter the condition, rich or poor, sick or healthy, free or imprisoned, he would consider it a blessing and be thankful for the opportunity and privilege to serve the Lord. Paul learned to be thankful no matter the condition. He knew the Lord was in control and God would give him the grace to overcome, which is why the Lord moved him to write in Romans 8:28: "And we know that all things work together for good to them that love God, to them who are the called according to his purpose."

From the time of Paul's salvation, he began to preach the gospel, and as soon as he did, the opposition came against him, and he was in rough terrain. Paul's life was in danger. The Jews attempted many times to falsely accuse and even murder him. Paul suffered not only from persecutions, but also with a health issue. The health issue was never made known but was referred to as "the thorn in the flesh." The diagnosis was believed to be ophthalmia, an inflammation of the eye and a condition that caused poor eyesight and headaches. Some people believe Paul had migraine headaches; nevertheless, Paul had an issue, and it was a burden to him. I can only imagine dealing with this misery. Of course, my wife says I'm a big baby because I cannot even handle the common cold. Many people have health issues. Paul went to the Lord in prayer about his issue, as we all should. He writes to the Corinthian church,

> And lest I should be exalted above measure through the abundance of the revelations, there was given to me a thorn in the flesh, the messenger of Satan to buffet me, lest I should be exalted above measure. For this thing I besought the Lord thrice, that it might depart from me. And he said unto me, My grace is sufficient for thee: for my strength is made perfect in weakness. Most gladly therefore will I rather glory in my infirmities, that the power of Christ may rest upon me. (2 Cor. 12:7–9)

God always answers the prayers of His children. Sometimes the answer is yes, sometimes it is no, and sometimes it is wait. But He always answers. Paul didn't necessarily get the answer for which he was looking. He went to the Lord three times, and God blessed him with a *no*. That *no* taught Paul that the Lord's grace was good enough and that the Lord would be with him. God would not remove the mountain or the valley but would give him the strength to climb and would hold his hand all the way through. By dealing with his weakness, Paul was able to see God's strength. He goes on to write in verse 10, "Therefore I take pleasure in infirmities, in reproaches, in necessities, in persecutions, in distresses for Christ's sake: for when I am weak, then I am strong." Not all blessings seem good at the time, nor are they always what we think they ought to be; but when we have the right heart and put them in his hands, God can use them to strengthen us, as He did with Paul.

I am reminded of the great hymn writer Fanny Crosby. When she was only six weeks old, she developed an eye inflammation. The doctor who treated her made a mistake, causing her blindness for life. She later wrote in a biography that if she could meet that doctor again, she would thank him for making her blind. In fact, she said she would not trade that blindness for anything. When she was younger, Fanny may have thought her blindness to be a weakness and a thorn in her flesh, but God used it to make her strong. Fanny wrote her first poem as a young child and went on to write thousands of songs to glorify her Savior. The issue we face isn't as important as how we face the issue. God doesn't always answer our prayers the way we want, but He knows best and gives us the grace to overcome.

As He walked the earth, our Savior, the Lord Jesus Christ, was a poor peasant. Born in a stall, He was wrapped in grave clothes and laid in a feed trough. During His ministry, He had no place to lay His head. Jesus stood and spoke the truth and was hated by the religious elite. He was a threat to their position and power; therefore, they set out to destroy him. Jesus tells us in John 15:25b, "They hated me without a cause." They were looking for the Messiah who was born in a palace, not a barn; a man of great position, not a peasant. They wanted a mighty warrior to destroy Rome and all their enemies, not a servant to seek and save that which was lost and to give his life on a Roman cross to pay for their sins and the sins of their enemies. They wanted a message of health, wealth, and prosperity, not one of truth and not the message that they were sinners and needed to be saved. Therefore, they rejected their Messiah because God's ways are not man's ways. They missed that promised Messiah. They hated him without a cause.

Christians are saved from the world. We are no longer a part of it. Satan is the god of this world. He is the enemy of God and our enemy as well. Jesus says in John 15:18, "If the world hate you, ye know that it hated me before it hated you." When we stand for the things of God throughout our Christian lives, we will be ridiculed and persecuted by the world because the things of God are foolishness to the natural man. When we stand for truth even in the land of the free, we are referred to as bigots and by many other names, but it is comforting to know that our Savior was hated even before we were. He will be with us every step of the way through the Holy Spirit. Of course, our attitude has a lot to do with many reactions we receive. We can offend someone by belittling them and having a holier-than-thou attitude that strikes a nerve. Some people will be offended no matter what you say or how you say it, but you should go with a heart of love. The goal is to bring others to Christ, not drive them further away.

Solomon, the wise man, said in Proverbs 25:11, "A word fitly spoken is like apples of gold in pictures of silver." I am reminded of the phrase used many times by a preacher friend of mine: "Be strong, but stay sweet." And what about the great love chapter, 1 Corinthians 13, to sum it all up! Whatever I do, no matter how great, without charity or love, it is worthless. We should neither cower in fear of offending someone with the truth nor accept or embrace sinful lifestyles. Jesus was the perfect example. He came with love and meekness, yet He stood with authority. It was that perfect balance. When Christ came, He truly desired repentance. Sometimes He spoke softly. At other times, He was downright harsh, but being God, He was perfect in every way, and everything was done in love. Jesus says in John 15:19, "If ye were of the world, the world would love his own: but because ye are not of the world, but I have chosen you out of the world, therefore the world hateth you." Jesus said we are chosen of Him and we belong to Him; therefore, we are hated by the world.

Let me use two examples of the chosen being hated. The first is the chosen wife of Jehovah. God made Abraham a promise that He would make him a great nation. Through that nation, all of the families of the earth will be blessed. That nation is the little nation of Israel. Through Israel, we have the Law of Moses; the Old Testament scriptures; the Word of God; and, finally, the Savior of the world, the Lord Jesus Christ. Israel is God's chosen people. They rejected the chosen Messiah, the Lord Jesus Christ. He was hated and crucified by His very own people; therefore, God scattered them throughout the world. God hasn't forgotten his promise to Abraham. In fact, nearly two thousand years later, He has brought the Israelites back into that chosen land, the land He promised to Abraham. One day the Lord Jesus Christ will reign in Jerusalem and set up His kingdom as God's promise will be fulfilled. All nations in existence at that time will come to Jerusalem to worship the true king. Today, after being almost completely wiped out many times throughout the centuries, the Israelites have come back into that land and become one of our most powerful allies. Of course, as you notice, they are hated by the majority of the nations with many saying they have no right to exist. Why? Because they are chosen of God and are hated without a cause.

The second example is the bride of Christ. After the rejection of their Messiah, God set the Jews aside. This was the beginning of the age of grace, the church age. Jesus tells a parable in Luke 14:16. To paraphrase, a man prepared a great supper for his friends. When the supper was ready, he called them to the feast, but each had other plans and rejected the invitation. This is the picture of the nation of Israel. The man then decided to go out into the streets and call any-one who would come. Many of the lame, sick, and poor came to the feast. The man then saw there was room for more, so he sent to call more. One by one they came to the great supper. This is a picture of the Gentiles, the body of believers known as the church.

Jesus continues to call today as He has called for the last two thousand years, and there is still more room. During this time of the gospel message, Christians have been persecuted, tortured, and killed for the cause of Christ. Many Christians were killed by the Roman Catholic Church because they believed the scriptures had the final authority rather than the church and the pope. Persecution had been widespread throughout the world until the founding of America, a nation built on biblical principles and the freedom of religion. Unfortunately, we, as a nation, have turned from God; and persecution is now on our very shores. The nation's foundation and the constitution, which were based on the scriptures, are despised. Prayer is no longer allowed in our schools. The Bible is offensive, and the name of God can no longer be used, unless it is used in vain. The Ten Commandments have been taken from public places, and Lord help us if we display a cross. There is a movement for freedom from religion. Persecution is here, and it will only get worse in time. Jesus warns in Mark 13:9,

> But take heed to yourselves: for they shall deliver you up to councils; and in the synagogues ye shall be beaten: and ye shall be brought before rulers and kings for my sake, for a testimony against them.

The church is not of this world; therefore, it is also hated without a cause.

"Then said Jesus unto his disciples, If any man will come after me, let him deny himself, and take up his cross, and follow me" (Matt. 16:24). An object of death, the cross was used to carry out punishment, the death penalty by the Romans in that day. The criminals would be hung on a cross just outside of town on the main road in and out. They would hang for several days, even after death. Everyone who passed by was reminded of the consequences of breaking the law. The cross is a symbol of death and suffering. When a criminal was hung on the cross, a spike was driven through each wrist since a person's hands really don't have any way to support weight. With the arms stretched out, the weight of the body would be on the wrists. The person would then continually push up on his toes to ease the pain and allow him to gasp for breath. During this time, the centurions would occasionally beat or spear the person, torturing him on the cross. As time went on, his head would fall forward and cut off the air supply, causing suffocation. Sometimes in order to speed up the process, the centurions would come through and break the two legs to make the person suffocate quicker. After hours, or possibly even days, of suffering, if the person was still alive, the birds would come and pluck their eyes and continue eating their flesh. The smell of death would be strong along the edge of the city. This was a gruesome form of death. There is nothing rosy about a cross. It is an offense. Jesus suffered on a cross for your sins and mine, and He commands, "Take up your cross and follow me!" Have you taken up your cross for the service of Christ?

What does it mean to take up one's cross? And how would one go about achieving this great task in the first place? It's easy to look at Matthew 16:24, focus completely on taking up our cross, and miss the most important part of this verse thereby taking it out of context. The Lord begins with a choice: "If any man will come after me." Jesus said, "Come unto me." God is not willing that any should perish but that all should come unto repentance. The Spirit and the church say come to the Savior. Jesus is calling. Have you heeded the call? The first step in carrying one's cross is believing in Jesus Christ and trusting Him as personal Savior. Once we come to Jesus as Savior, we are commanded to deny ourselves. Denying oneself is complete surrender. I am amazed by how many people profess to be Christians and yet never surrender to follow Him in complete obedience. We live in immoral times. Even though adultery and fornication (living with one outside of marriage) and homosexuality are acceptable in our society, these are sins in the eyes of God. Unless there is repentance, there is no surrender. John the Baptist said to bring forth fruits of repentance. In other words, show your faith by your actions. If you are unwilling to turn from sin, there is no way you can truly follow Jesus. In fact, there is a chance you were never saved to begin with. Jesus bought us with a price, the price of His precious blood. We are no longer our own; we belong to him. As we looked at the heart of the bird dog, we saw our desire is to do His will, not our own. He is the center of our lives. In order to deny ourselves, we must be filled with the Holy Spirit, which God gives us when we are saved. The Holy Spirit not only gives us the power to deny ourselves, He also gives us the power to take up our cross of suffering and sacrifice, true service to Him. We don't take up our cross for salvation; we take it up for service.

Under Roman law, the one to be crucified would carry his own cross from the judgment hall to the place of the crucifixion. This act signified submission to Roman authority. Jesus led by example as He submitted to mankind, which was the will of God, and was obedient even unto death in order that He might pay for the sins of all mankind, as the innocent and perfect Lamb of God. What an example to us! Jesus never told us to do anything He wasn't willing to do Himself, and He never gave us a command He didn't give us the power and the ability to perform. We likewise are to take up our cross in submission to Him and be willing to sacrifice our very life, following Him no matter where He leads. Jesus goes on to say in Matthew 16:25, "For whosoever will save his life shall lose it: and whosoever will lose his life for my sake shall find it." This verse is a picture of a servant carrying his cross, a faith so great it produces action by denying and suffering while following our Lord and Savior Jesus Christ.

Many people today and throughout history have attempted to carry their own cross without first coming to Christ in salvation; therefore, they have failed as time went on. The cross is difficult to carry since it is a symbol of suffering, shame, persecution, and death. Sure, many people seem to carry it for a while under their own strength. Some people, because of personality, can go much longer than others; but through time and testing, it becomes too heavy to bear alone. As Christians, we cannot bear the cross alone; but with the help of the Spirit, we can stop, get another grip on that cross, and carry on until the Lord calls us home.

During our Lord's ministry, He gained a large following. Many people saw His miracles and listened to His teaching. One day Jesus had been teaching in a desert place, and it was getting late. The people were hungry, and Jesus asked if anyone had food. Andrew brought a young lad to Christ. The boy had five loaves of bread and two small fish, but what is that among so many? Of course, our Lord can take a little or nothing at all and make an abundance. Jesus fed five thousand people that day with enough leftovers to feed His disciples. Every person's hunger was satisfied. Because of this great miracle, the five thousand desired to make him king. They realized that through Jesus and His power, they could not only be healed when they were sick but also could be filled and never hunger. They knew Jesus could destroy their enemies, so they took up their crosses and followed Him. They were seeking for Christ to meet their temporal, physical needs and desires. Jesus calls them out in John 6:26 and says, "Verily, verily, I say unto you, Ye seek me, not because ye saw the miracles, but because ye did eat of the loaves, and were filled." They took up their crosses and followed Him for personal gain, the things that will perish.

Many people today have taken up their crosses for what they can get in life, hoping He will meet their every need and give them their hearts' worldly desires, including the lusts of their flesh. Instead of denying themselves, they are serving themselves. To these people, Christ is like a genie in a bottle. Jesus adds in verse 27, "Labour not for the meat which perisheth, but for that meat which endureth unto everlasting life, which the Son of man shall give unto you." In other words, we should seek things that are eternal. Seek first the kingdom of God and His righteousness, seek Him in salvation, and seek the rewards we will one day receive by denying ourselves and serving Him with all of our hearts. Because of their unbelief, these people continued to carry their crosses under the power of their own weak flesh. The followers then asked the age-old question: "What must we do to do the works of God?" The works that our Lord performed could only be done by the power of God. Nicodemus realized this fact as he came to Jesus by night in John 3. When we come to Jesus in salvation, we are given the power to do His works by His spirit. Man has attempted to somehow work his way into favor with God since the days of Cain and Abel when Cain brought the works of his hands as a sacrifice and God rejected him. These followers desire to be self-sufficient, but no one has ever been saved by denying oneself or by taking up their cross, nor could one ever truly follow Christ unless they first answered the call to come to Jesus and put their faith and trust in Him and His finished work on Calvary's cross for salvation. Many people today are carrying a cross to be saved. Jesus said to carry your cross because you are saved and that's the only way.

Jesus gained a great following when the people saw the miracles and especially when He fed them in the desert place. These followers were enjoying the blessings of God. They were gaining faith that Jesus would take care of them as a political leader, going as far as desiring to make Him their king, but a faith that cannot the tested cannot be trusted. It was time to find out on what their faith was based. Was it based on truly believing that Jesus was the Christ, the Son of God? Was it based on personal gain? Was their faith based on the temporal things that perish or maybe the good feeling that comes through good works and deeds as they attempt to work their way into favor with God? They were following in the wrong way and for all the wrong reasons; therefore, Jesus had to test their faith.

He went on to teach a great message. "And Jesus said unto them, I am the bread of life: he that cometh to me shall never hunger; and he that believeth on me shall never thirst" (John 6:35). Many of the followers at this time were not true believers. They picked up their crosses but were not fully committed to carry them all the way. Jesus then said in verse 36, "But I said unto you, that ye also have seen me, and believe not." Because of their unbelief and to test their faith, Jesus taught a message that only a true believer could understand.

> I am the living bread which came down from heaven: If any man eat of this bread, he shall live forever: and the bread that I will give is my flesh, which I will give for the life of the world. (John 6:51)

The Bible is to be taken literally, but there are times when it can only be used in the spiritual sense. This text is a prime example. I think we can all agree that Jesus was not into cannibalism. He would in no way advise one to eat his flesh, so this text must be taken spiritually, not literally. What did Jesus say? "If any man shall eat of this bread he shall live forever."

To understand this verse, let's go to the Last Supper, or what we observe today as the Communion supper.

> And as they were eating, Jesus took bread, and blessed it, and brake it, and gave it to the disciples, and said, Take, eat; this is my body. And he took the cup, and gave thanks, and gave it to them, saying, Drink ye all of it; For this is my blood of the new testament, which is shed for many for the remission of sins. (Matt. 26:26–28)

Jesus took bread and said, "This is my body." Was it really His literal body? Of course not! It was a symbol of His body that He gave as a sacrifice for our sins. In John 6:51, He said, "The bread that I will give is my flesh, which I will give for the life of the world." Once again His flesh, or body, was given for the life of the world. At the Last Supper, Jesus also took the cup of wine, or juice; gave them to drink; and said, "This is my blood—drink ye all of it." Christ had to give His body and shed His blood to pay for the sins of the world for "without the shedding of blood there is no remission" (Heb. 9:22b).

We continue this practice of Communion in our churches today. Why? The answer is found in 1 Corinthians 11:26: "For as often as ye eat this bread, and drink this cup, ye do shew the Lord's death till he come." This practice is a symbol of what He has done for us on the cross of Calvary. In 1 Corinthians 11:24–25, both verses end with the same statement: this do "in remembrance of me." This is so we never forget and will be continually reminded that as we carry our crosses, Jesus carried a far heavier cross than you and I could ever bear. In John 6:51 the message was the same. Jesus said He would give His flesh, or His body, and His blood. To eat means to partake, or receive, the gift of salvation. The words *eat* and *drink* are in the Greek aorist tense, which means "once for all." Jesus came once for all, and by receiving Him as Savior, we are saved once for all. Because of their unbelief, the Jews could not understand. Therefore, they took it the wrong way. In John 6:52, we read, "The Jews therefore strove among themselves, saying, How can this man give us his flesh to eat?" Again in verse 60, "Many therefore of his disciples, when they had heard this, said, This is an hard saying; who can hear it?" Finally, in verse 66, "From that time many of his disciples went back, and walked no more with him." They laid their crosses down and walked away. Why? Because of their unbelief. They followed Jesus because He made them feel good. He showed them power they never experienced before, and He fed them when they were physically hungry. But then came the message that man is starving spiritually and in need of the bread of life; that man is a sinner, dead in trespasses and sin, helpless and hopeless; and his works are worthless before God. Because of man's state, Jesus must give His body, shed His blood, and die on a cross to pay for the sins of the world; and every man, woman, boy, and girl must "eat," or receive and accept that gift of salvation, or spend eternity in a place called hell, where they will be tormented for eternity.

John 3:16 is therefore one of the greatest promises ever given to man: "For God so loved the world, that he gave his only begotten Son, that whosoever believeth in him should not perish, but have everlasting life." God's love, God's mercy, and God's grace. "I love you so much, take my body, take my blood," He pleaded. That is the only way to salvation, but they said they didn't like the preaching. It's too hard, it's offensive, it hurts my feelings. I want someone to make me feel good when they preach, not point out my sins. The Holy Spirit might bring you under conviction, then you would have to acknowledge that you're a sinner and have to repent of your sins. People are laying down their crosses left and right and turning away from the truth to fables for this very reason: first, because of their unbelief; second, because they want a message of prosperity, not revival. They enjoy the blessings of God, but they despise the Word of God. Is your preacher stepping on your toes today? Does the Lord convict you of sin during the message? Don't lay down your cross and turn to another message. Believe, come to Jesus, deny yourself, then take up your cross and follow Him. Oh and by the way, thank that preacher who had the gumption to point his finger and preach the truth without turning one way or the other. We need more of them, and they need encouragement.

After many cleared the area, Jesus asked the twelve in John 6:67, "Will ye also go away?" Simon Peter, being the spokesman of the group, confessed in verses 68–69, "Lord, to whom shall we go? Thou hast the words of eternal life. And we believe and are sure that thou art that Christ, the Son of the living God." This was Peter's great confession. Have you made that confession today? Is Jesus Lord of your life? The twelve disciples got another grip on their crosses and continued on the path forward following their Lord.

Jesus proclaimed that one of his disciples was a devil. He knew one would betray him. Peter spoke for the twelve. They all believed that Jesus was that Messiah; perhaps even Judas believed. The problem with Judas and with many professed Christians today is they believe with their heads, not with their hearts. James tells us, "Thou believest that there is one God; thou doest well: the devils also believe, and tremble" (James 2:19). When we believe with our minds, we walk by sight. When we believe with our hearts, we walk by faith. The Word of God tells us to walk by faith, not by sight. Judas walked by sight; therefore, he desired what he could see: personal gain, prosperity, and position. Remember Jesus said, "You cannot serve two masters, because you will love one and hate the other."

As we look at Judas, we see he loved money. Therefore he hated the Lord. In 1 Timothy 6:10, we read, "For the love of money is the root of all evil: which while some coveted after, they have erred from the faith, and pierced themselves through with many sorrows." Judas was more concerned with money than the mission of Christ. In John 12, Jesus went to a supper with friends Mary, Martha, and Lazarus. As they sat to eat, Mary brought out a pound of spikenard, a very expensive ointment, and began to anoint the feet of Jesus. Judas responded in John 12:5, "Why was not this ointment sold for three hundred pence, and given to the poor?" Of course, John wrote this gospel about fifty years after the fact, so already knowing the outcome, he commented, "This he said, not that he cared for the poor; but because he was a thief, and had the bag, and bare what was put therein." Having the bag meant that Judas was the treasurer, and being identified as a thief, he evidently planned to keep the money for himself.

I feel like all the teaching of turning the other cheek and being a servant and the fact that Jesus was going away and they had to be patient wore on Judas, testing his faith. Like many of the Jews, he expected the Messiah to come and destroy all their enemies. He was for the here and now. It was about what was in it for him. He wasn't concerned about others. He had gotten to the point that this was a dead-end road for him and he was going to cut his losses, make a little money and bail.

> Then one of the twelve, called Judas Iscariot, went unto the chief priests, And said unto them, What will you give me, and I will deliver him unto you? And they covenanted with him for thirty pieces of silver. And from that time he sought opportunity to betray him. (Matt. 26:14–16)

Judas saw an opportunity to turn this into a profitable situation. Of course, Jesus already knew his heart. You cannot hide from God. As they sat down to eat the Last Supper, Jesus announced that one of them would betray Him. Each one sorrowfully asked, "Lord, is it I?" They were truly concerned. No one wanted to betray Christ, except the plan had already been laid. Jesus gave Judas a chance as He warned him of the consequences. "The Son of man goeth as it is written of him: but woe unto that man by whom the Son of man is betrayed! it had been good for that man if he had not been born" (Matt. 26:24).

Judas rejected Jesus as Lord, but he could have repented. He still had a choice; but his love for money, for instant gratification, was greater than his love for the Lord. "Then said Jesus unto him, That thou doest do quickly" (John 13:27b). Judas's mind was already made up. There was no turning back, so he laid down his cross. He sold his cross and his Messiah for thirty pieces of silver, the price of a slave. We live in a day where money reigns: people minister for personal gain, and many preachers see financial opportunities in the ministry. How many men would preach for nothing? What about you who give every Sunday faithfully? If you couldn't write it off for a tax deduction, would you still give or give the same amount? How about this, do you serve the Lord to gain a good feeling because it helps you emotionally or for what you can get from the Lord, or are you serving for what you can give to the Lord? What happens when the pay gets cut, the tax break is taken away, or the emotion is no longer there? Will you be like Judas and lay down your cross and walk away?

One more laid down his cross, and now there are eleven. That night after Judas had gone his way and supper was over, Jesus quoted a prophecy from Zechariah 13:7. "All ye shall be offended because of me this night: for it is written, I will smite the shepherd, and the sheep of the flock shall be scattered abroad" (Matt. 26:31). Jesus warned them that they, out of fear, would leave him; but Peter, with boldness and courage, proclaimed in verse 33, "Though all men shall be offended because of thee, yet will I never be offended." Peter claimed no matter the cost that he would carry his cross and stand to the death. Jesus replied to Peter, "Before the rooster crows, you will deny me three times." We get the account in Matthew 26:47–50:

> And while he yet spake, lo, Judas one of the twelve, came, and with him a great multitude with swords and staves, from the chief priest and elders of the people. Now he that betrayed him gave them a sign, saying, "Whomsoever I shall kiss, that same is he: hold him fast." And forthwith he came to Jesus, and said, "Hail, master; and kissed him." And Jesus said unto him, "Friend, wherefore art thou come?" Then came they, and laid hands on Jesus, and took him. And behold, one of them which were with Jesus stretched out his hand, and drew his sword, and struck a servant of the high priest's, and smote off his ear.

Peter stood strong by having the courage to fight for the Lord, but I would have to question his judgment as he was getting ready to take on an army with a knife. Had this been a sword as we think of, it probably would have cut down into his shoulder or possibly severed his jugular vein and caused him to bleed to death. Also I don't know what area Peter was aiming for, but the ear doesn't seem to be the best target. Of course, I don't want to give Peter a hard time. A grouse just flew out in front of me, and I blew the branch out of a tree. I didn't even come close to bringing down the bird. It happens to the best of us.

Jesus didn't need Peter's defense anyway. He could have called twelve legions of angels to destroy the world and set Him free, but He chose to die for you and me. Matthew 26:56b tells us as Jesus was led away, "Then all the disciples forsook him, and fled." They laid down their crosses and ran, leaving Jesus alone to defend Himself. These eleven disciples had believed, they had truly come to Jesus, they had denied themselves and taken up their crosses and followed Jesus. Unfortunately, just like the disciples, we are weak in the flesh and often fall short, even as Christians. Two disciples, Peter and John, followed from a distance. They hadn't completely laid down their crosses; they just kind of dragged them behind. We pick this part of the story up in Luke 22:54–62:

> Then took they him, and led him, and brought him into the high priests house. And Peter followed afar off. And when they had kindled a fire in the midst of the hall, and were sat down together, Peter sat down among them. But a certain maid beheld him as he sat by the fire, and earnestly looked upon him, and said, This man was also with him. And he denied him, saying, Woman, I know him not. And after a little while another saw him, and said, Thou art also of them. And Peter said, Man, I am not. And about the space of one hour after another confidently affirmed, saying, Of a truth this fellow also was

with him: for he is a Galilean. And Peter said,
Man, I know not what thou sayest. And immediately, while he yet spake, the cock crew. And the
Lord turned, and looked upon Peter. And Peter
remembered the word of the Lord, how he had
said unto him, before the cock crow, thou shalt
deny me thrice. And Peter went out, and wept
bitterly.

Peter's life was in danger. He was afraid of persecution, so he
laid down his cross. After he denied the Lord, he was reminded by
the crow of a rooster and was cut to the heart. He went out and wept
bitterly. Peter was ashamed. He had let down his friend, his mentor,
and his Lord. Now, more than ever, Christians need to stand for
the things of God and not be ashamed. Persecution is nothing new.
Christians have been decapitated, tortured, and even burned alive
for the cause of Christ. Today in America, we may not face such
persecutions as the ones mentioned, but it is getting worse. As time
goes on, many people will lay down their crosses and deny the Lord
out of fear, as Peter did. John tells us in 1 John 2:28, "And now, little children, abide in him; that, when he shall appear, we may have
confidence, and not be ashamed before him at his coming." Abiding
in Christ through the Holy Spirit is the only way we can overcome
and carry our crosses.

Finally, at the cross, as Jesus hangs in agony, knowing His friends
have betrayed Him and fled, He looks down and sees four women,
one being his mother, and John, His beloved disciple. When John
wrote the Gospel of John, he never referred to himself by name but
always as "that disciple" or "the one whom Jesus loved." John never
laid down his cross; he followed Jesus all the way. Many disciples laid
down their crosses because they didn't like the message. Judas laid
down his cross because he desired the things of this world. Peter and
nine others laid down their crosses because they were afraid. Only
John was left. Grounded in strong biblical faith, John was the one
who was abiding in Christ. He committed himself for the cause of
Christ. John was rewarded for his faith as he was the last disciple to

die. Although he was held in prison, he died of old age. James was beheaded, and Peter was later crucified.

With our Lord, we have forgiveness and the opportunity to pick up our cross once again and carry on. As Christians, we lay down our cross because of sin. We have already believed, so laying down our cross is not laying down salvation. Taking up our cross is service because we are saved. John tells us when we confess our sins, He is faithful and just to forgive us our sins and cleanse us from all unrighteousness. Peter later repented of his sin and picked his up his cross once again, and by the power of the Holy Spirit, he preached the greatest sermon ever preached with three thousand people being saved. James wrote one of the most practical Epistles for the glory of God, so yes, there is forgiveness if we are saved by His grace. We can pick up our cross once again and continue to follow Him. The most important question to answer is, Have you come to Jesus in salvation? Then have you denied yourself and taken up your cross and followed Him? Are you still carrying your cross, or have you laid it down along the way because it seems too heavy? As the time draws nearer to the coming of our Savior, that cross will get heavier, we will get tired, and we will wonder how much longer. But our Lord will give us strength. "I can do all things through Christ which strengtheneth me" (Phil. 4:13).

As I move through these thick briars, though tough, it seems to have paid off. Yes, I missed one, but it flew down into more open territory. The briars continue to scratch and poke, the limbs continue to fly back in my face, and the rocks slip out from under my feet; so I grip my shotgun a little tighter. I keep my head down. I can see better terrain ahead. As a Christian, I have the Holy Spirit. My heart won't be troubled as Satan hurls his darts at me and the world continues to ridicule, but by the Word of God, I know there is a light at the end of the tunnel. So I grip my cross a little tighter because He has promised me peace with Him for all eternity.

COMRADERY

As we move out of the heavy cover, I see a small spring covered with hawthorn trees and briars. Maddie, who is about twenty-five yards from me, is moving in the opposite direction. Turning toward the spring, I think, *This looks like a pretty good place for one of the grouse that we jumped earlier to hide.* Although Maddie is a good ways off, she is constantly in tune with my movements. As I turn left, Maddie circles around in front of me; and when I turn right, she swings to my right, allowing us to cover large areas and the dog to do the hunting and find the bird. This is the joy of hunting with a bird dog. It is the relationship and friendship. It's working together as a team. It's the comradery.

A grouse seems to be near. Maddie begins to get excited, her tail speed picks up, and she begins to move faster back and forth with her nose to the ground. Suddenly, she freezes on point. The point is the natural reaction of a pointing dog—the action before it pounces on its prey, but the bird dog is trained not to pounce but to hold. She has done her job. Now it's my turn to move in, flush, and shoot the bird. Once the bird goes down, it is Maddie's job to go and fetch. That is assuming I don't miss, which I've been known to do. Okay, let's be honest, I have a zero-to-three streak going here, but we won't dwell on that ratio.

Some trainers will work a bird dog puppy on a bird wing. This should, of course, be used in moderation as the dog can become dependent on sight rather than smell. The handler puts a grouse or quail wing on a fishing rod and floats it out in front of the puppy. The puppy then points the wing. The puppy is never allowed to catch the wing thereby learning to hold. As the puppy matures in areas where there aren't many wild birds, pen-raised quail or chukars are a good method of training. The only drawbacks are birds that are not good fliers. The most damaging thing to a bird dog is if it catches the bird. It is the dog's job to find and point the bird, and it's the hunter's job to shoot the bird. The hunter depends on the dog, and the dog depends on the hunter. They are a team. If the dog realizes it can catch the bird on its own, the relationship is broken. The dog becomes self-centered. Focusing only on himself and what is best for him, the dog will flush the birds and try to catch them before the hunter has a chance. This is a very frustrating situation, and it defeats the purpose of having a dog. The hunter can no longer trust or depend on the dog until this habit is broken. The dog must once again realize that he can't do it on his own; he must depend on his master.

The Christian life is no different. It is a life of dependence. From the time of salvation, we trust Jesus and Him alone. Jesus paid the price for our sins on the cross. We have the choice to accept or reject His finished work. By accepting His sacrifice, we are fully depending on Him to save us. If people add anything to salvation, such as their own works of righteousness—the mindset that "I can do enough good works to find favor with God"—they are depending on themselves and becoming self-centered, making it impossible to do anything to please the Lord. We depend on the Lord for salvation, but we also depend on Him to meet our daily needs of life. Our God is an awesome, almighty, gracious God. He created this world and sustains or holds everything in place. He gives us the sunshine and the rain, which yields the abundance of crops and food for us to eat. He gives us air to breath and the ability to do so. It is because of Him that we have homes in which to live and warm clothes on our backs. He has blessed us with knowledge and the abilities to learn and to build. For all these great blessings, we can go to Him in thanksgiving, for it is He who gives and on whom we depend. It is impossible for us to do anything on our own without Him. Our loving Father in heaven wants us to depend, look to, and trust in Him for all of our needs. I am reminded of Proverbs 3:5: "Trust in the LORD with all thine heart; and lean not unto thine own understanding." To trust is to commit, to fully depend on the Lord, not our own wisdom for our own desires. Verse 6 goes on to say, "In all thy ways acknowledge him, and he shall direct thy paths." When we fully depend with all of our hearts and acknowledge His will, plan, and purpose for our lives, then we can have confidence He will direct our paths.

When God saved us, He gave us a mission. We must fully depend on Him to meet our needs and equip us with the tools and ability to accomplish that mission. Maddie was equipped through nature by breeding to do her job. I am equipped with a 20-gauge shotgun to do mine and to accomplish the purpose we are out here to fulfill. For any mission God calls us to do, He likewise will certainly give us the ability to fulfill that mission.

I am reminded of the many times in Scripture when God made a promise or called someone to do something that literally seemed impossible, yet as they depended on God, they were able to perform those impossible tasks. One who depended on God even though the promise seemed impossible was Abraham, the father of many nations, the patriarch of Israel. Abraham was known as the friend of God. He was called by God to leave his family and go to a place that he had never seen. God promised that He would make him a great nation and that all the families of the earth would be blessed through his seed. Abraham was living a successful life where he was. He and wife Sarah were getting above their childbearing years; but by faith, Abraham believed God, followed His call, and fully depended on Him. Throughout Abraham's life, God blessed Abraham with much wealth, but there was one thing missing. Abraham had no children. All he had was a house full of servants and, as you and I might think, empty promises. Sarah was barren. She couldn't have children.

When Abraham was in his mid-eighties, his faith began to waver, and he decided to take things into his own hands. He was like a bird dog on point, waiting on his master; but he just couldn't wait any longer, pouncing toward the bird, watching it fly away, missing the opportunity, and losing the blessing. Abraham decided to marry Sarah's Egyptian servant Hagar and have children through her. Hagar gave birth to Ishmael, bringing jealousy and havoc into his own house. God said wait and depend on Him, but Abraham had to learn that valuable lesson. Finally, fifteen years later, when Abraham was one hundred years old, God fulfilled his promise through Sarah, who was at the age of ninety. Because of Abraham's learned patience, he received the great blessing of a son. However, because of his previous impatience, he would suffer the consequence of havoc in his household, a havoc that continues throughout the Middle East today.

God gave Abraham a son, Isaac, through whom He would fulfill a great promise and blessing. It was through him God gave birth to the great nation of Israel. It was through him God gave the Law and the one who came to fulfill that Law, our Savior, Jesus Christ, reminding us of the promise, "In thee shall all of the nations of the earth be blessed." In the day of instant gratification, it is hard for us to wait on anything, much less the Lord. You and I just as easily can become impatient and even neglect to seek the Lord's will. It's like the old saying, "My way or the highway." We pounce on what seems right in our own eyes rather than wait on our Lord. This action causes us missed opportunities and missed blessings, which the Lord has in store for each of His children.

To Christians, God is saying, "Wait on me, depend on me, I love you, I know what is best for you, and I have a plan for your life, and by depending on me, I will meet your needs and bless you richly."

When we put our faith in Jesus Christ as our Savior, we are placed into a body of believers known as the church. Paul tells us in 1 Corinthians 12:13, "For by one Spirit are we all baptized into one body..." The word *baptized* simply means "to be placed into." This one body is the church, not the local church and not denominational. The church is made up of those people who put their faith and trust in Jesus Christ for salvation! This is the future bride of Christ. The church, being made up of believers, is a body of individuals depending on Jesus Christ for salvation. Each member is a part of the body. We depend on Christ for life, and we depend on the Holy Spirit and each other to serve His purpose for the glory of God. We are the body. Christ is the head. Paul used the human body as an example of the church in 1 Corinthians 12:12–14:

> For as the body is one, and hath many members, and all the members of that one body, being many, are one body: so also is Christ. For

by one Spirit are we all baptized into one body, whether we be Jews or Gentiles, whether we be bond or free; and have been all made to drink into one Spirit. For the body is not one member, but many.

The human body is amazing. It is so intricately designed by our Creator. Each part is made with precision with all the parts working together and depending on one another. The internal parts keep the body alive and give energy and growth, the legs move the body, the arms and hands serve as tools for the body, and the five senses benefit the body. Paul wrote to the Corinthian church, which was having problems. To paraphrase, there were many people fighting over doing the same job in the church, while others (much like our churches today) didn't want to do anything at all. Imagine if you had five arms. Now I must say there are times it seems I could use more than the two arms I have, but then I'm sure they would just get in the way. Suppose you have five arms and one leg. They would put you out of balance and hinder you from functioning as God planned. In the church, we can also have too many people doing one task while neglecting other principle duties in the church. If you went to a church where everyone was a Sunday school teacher, who would listen? Who would you teach? Suppose in that church there was no one to do the music or take up the offering.

God gives each of us gifts in the church. We must seek the Lord's will and then depend on Him to show us our gift so we can do our part in the body. Paul says in 1 Corinthians 12:31, "But covet earnestly the best gifts: and yet shew I unto you a more excellent way." There can be too many with the same part in the church, but there can also be too few. What if your legs don't work or your fingers and hands cannot move or you can no longer see with your eyes or hear with your ears. We call those handicaps, and they hinder the body from functioning at its fullest potential. These things happen regularly in the church today as many members are not doing their part, or even showing up. They are missing in action. When an amputee loses a body part, that part is useless to the body. The body, being an example of the church, shows that each member depends on other members; and we all depend on the Lord, who is the head for His plan and purpose.

Have you ever stubbed your toe, broken a bone, or had a toothache? These small things can affect the whole body and make it less productive. Think about the little part inside your ears called the eardrum. When the eardrum has problems, the whole body can lose its balance, thus setting the body in disarray. When one member suffers, the whole body suffers. Paul writes in 1 Corinthians 12:26, "And whether one member suffer, all the members suffer with it; or one member be honoured, all the members rejoice with it." God designed the members of the body to depend on each other. He designed the church so that we depend on one another. When one suffers, we all suffer, and when the Lord blesses a member, there is no jealousy or bitterness, and we all rejoice.

We owe our gratitude to the many soldiers who have willingly sacrificed so much for the freedoms we enjoy. Some have gone to battle and returned as amputees because of their sacrifice. Many of those soldiers take years to adjust to their loss, with some struggling to the point they are willing to give up. There are others who refuse to give up. They continue to fight and reach down deep. They overcome that weakness with strength and perform as well as anyone else. Often the other parts make up for the missing part. In other words, one who has lost a right arm overcomes that loss with a stronger left arm or maybe uses their feet to overcome the loss of the arm. What happens in the local church when one of the deacons steps down, the pastor suddenly leaves, the choir director falls ill, or the church splits and those people you depend on are no longer there? Does the church quit? Do you cancel the services? No! The parts that are left, by the power of the Holy Spirit, step up and fulfill the duties of the ones who are missing. Then there are those parts that seem so insignificant: the little toes and fingers. Such small parts yet they play a large role in the function of the body. In the church, there are those people who are younger or older and not able to get out like they once did. There are people who sit in the pews Sunday after Sunday and you don't hear much from them. They don't preach or teach, but they are faithful. Many of those people are prayer warriors. They have the ear of God, and without them, the teacher doesn't teach and the preacher doesn't preach. Although they seem insignificant, they play a large part in the services behind the scenes. We depend on those people and don't even realize it. The church is a body depending on each other, dwelling in unity for the glory of our Lord. The words of David still ring true today as he writes in Psalm 133:1, "Behold, how good and how pleasant it is for brethren to dwell together in unity!"

Maddie and I are a team depending on each other. When I was about five years old, my dad was a high school coach for football, basketball, and baseball. I rarely missed a game. I learned to love sports at an early age. Throughout sandlot years and high school, I participated in sports, but as I grew, football became my favorite. Football is a team sport with eleven players on the field at one time. Each player has an assignment, and each player depends on the other players to fulfill that assignment. As the old saying goes, "There is no 'I' in 'team.'" No one person can win a football game, no matter how talented they are. From what I have seen over the years, the talented shine because of the other ten players in the trenches. The quarterback is the leader. He calls and initiates the plays, but he cannot get the ball unless the center snaps it to him. The blockers block the defense, the runners run the ball, and receivers catch the ball. Suppose the linemen, the unsung heroes, decide not to block; the receivers are afraid to catch the ball; or the running back sees the defensive end coming at him and, in fear, throws the ball in the air and takes off in the other direction. Not only would the team fail, but also a coach might think those actions would be worthy of breaking a clipboard. Each player has an assignment and needs to learn the assignment well. Each player needs to have a desire to give his all, 110 percent, to score and win the game.

Preparation starts in the off season, the winter and summer months, before the games begin; and success follows when players are working out in the weight room and preparing their bodies to go into battle. As August approaches, the two-and three-a-day practices begin. At this time, the comradery, the unity of the team, begins to build. Players encourage one another. This toughest part of the season is when the quitters quit, the winners move on, and the players gel as a team. Plays are developed and learned in the classroom, and then it's back on the field to practice the plays in real time so that at game time the team is like a well-oiled machine with the ultimate goal of winning ball games. Repetition is key. Practice makes perfect. Hours go into plays, and timing is essential with handoffs and routes. But what if no one showed up for practice? How would each player or team as a whole perform? More than likely it would be a total failure and a loss, and the purpose of the team—to win ballgames—would not be fulfilled.

You may be happy with a participation trophy, but I would rather be the winner. I coached both of my sons' football teams from fourth through seventh grades. In the first year, they didn't win a game. They were like the Bad News Bears. They did much better in the second year. It seemed like we were making progress, but then in the third year, they again didn't win a game. One of the kids came up to me during practice at the end of the season and asked, "Coach Harman, are we getting trophies this year?"

I replied, "Young man, have you guys won a game yet?"

He said, "No."

So I responded, "Sorry, but rewards are earned. Go win some ball games, and we'll talk about trophies."

They didn't get a trophy that year, but the next year, they gelled as a team. Not only did they win every game, but also by game 3 only one team had gotten one first down and no one had scored on them. They dominated and earned a trophy that year.

Walking through these mountains and enjoying this great creation, I can worship God right here, and I have heard many others say the same, and even replace church with nature. Why should I go to church when I can worship here in the woods? The question is, what is the purpose of the local church? The church, a body of believers, not a building, is sent on the Great Commission by our Lord and Savior Jesus Christ in Matthew 28:18–20:

> And Jesus came and spake unto them, saying, "All power is given unto Me in heaven and in earth. Go ye therefore, and teach all nations, bap-

tizing them in the name of the Father, and of the
Son, and of the Holy Ghost: Teaching them to
observe all things whatsoever I have commanded
you: and, lo, I am with you always, even unto the
end of the world. Amen."

Jesus gave us a mission. Many people look at this as a call for a
missionary, but Jesus is calling all who believe to go. I heard a missionary put it plain and simple: When Jesus said, "Go," He is saying, "As you go." In other words, wherever you go—work, school,
recreation, everywhere—preach the gospel. The ultimate goal of the
church is to tell the good news that Jesus came and died for the sins
of the world and lead others to Christ. This is not a Sunday-morning,
Sunday-night, or Wednesday-night mission. It's a 24/7 mission that
never ends. What is the purpose for the church services? Isn't it a
time and place of worship? Yes, and when we worship in songs and
hymns, we praise God, but don't those hymns teach and encourage
us as we fulfill the mission? Music is powerful, and the music stays
with us even after the service is over. What about the teaching? The
more we learn of Jesus, the stronger our relationship becomes, and
the more we can tell others about Him. We learn how to live so that
we won't be a stumbling block to those people to whom we witness.
When we learn how to live, our lives themselves become witnesses for
Jesus Christ. What about fellowship and prayer? We learn to bond
with our brothers and sisters in Christ, and we learn to gel as we work
together on missions. We learn to pray for one another, bear one
another's burdens, and encourage one another as we give testimony
to our personal missions. You cannot get that in the forest.

It looks to me like church is where the team shows up for practice, but it is more than practice. Jesus said in Matthew 18:20, "For
where two or three are gathered together in my name, there am I in
the midst of them." In other words, when we show up to church, the
captain of the team, the Lord Himself, is right there joining with us
in fellowship. In the local church, the gospel is preached, but just as
important, believers are discipled and trained to take the gospel message out into the world, as well as to thank and praise our God for

what He has done for us and the privilege to serve Him. What kind of a team would we have if no one ever showed up to practice? No wonder Jesus warns us of being ashamed at His coming. We cannot get the proper training we need by walking through the forest. We are to take what we learn from the church service into the world. It is too bad many Christians want to be on the team but they don't want to show up for practice.

Sudden cardiac arrest (SCA) is the most common cause of death among young athletes, usually basketball and football players. Most cases are hereditary and caused by a weakness or some underlying and undetected problem in the heart. Unfortunately, by the time it is realized, it is too late. During stressful physical activity, the heart is overstressed and strained to the point of cardiac arrest, and the player dies there on the field or the court. Since it goes undetected, there is no real cure for this disease. I don't know if it has anything to do with the situation, but when I was younger and playing football, we had three practices a day in the late summer heat. Occasionally, you would hear of someone dying from heat exhaustion, but that was rare. At that time, practice was done in the heat of the day to prepare for the fourth quarter. (The team in the best shape usually will win a close game.) Teams don't practice like that anymore. When it's too hot, they practice at night when it is cooler. I just wonder if they are getting the preparation they need for game time. I think it is almost impossible to be completely prepared especially for that first game of the year, no matter how hard you practice. When the lights come on, the band is playing, fans are cheering, and you have the drive to win, the adrenaline is pumping, your heart is racing, and you push harder than you ever did in practice or preseason. You have to gain that extra yard, run a little faster, and push a little harder; and with an underlying problem, the heart is pushed to the limit causing SCA.

Not to take this lightly, but we, as Christians, called to the Great Commission, can never prepare for each scenario we will face. We can study, listen, learn, and pray; but until we actually go out to the battlefield, we don't know what we will face. There may also be an underlying problem in our relationship with Jesus Christ. We need to depend on the Holy Spirit and allow Him to work through us rather than going in our own strength. We may have unconfessed sin in our lives or be living a lifestyle of which we shouldn't be a part. These things can cause a strain or hindrance in our work for our Lord. When the pressure is put on and the Christian is tested to the fullest, they fail and become discouraged. They fall away, turning from the work of the Lord and no longer being the testimony they should be. We have the Holy Spirit within us. He prepares, teaches, and brings things to remembrance the things we study; but underlying problems quench the Spirit and make us of no effect. The more we prepare, the more we learn. We can see these underlying problems and deal with them before they cause problems in our service. Being spiritually fit by having a right relationship with our Savior through the Holy Spirit and allowing Him to be active in our lives gives us the power to fulfill the mission even under great pressure.

Cancer seems to be one of the most feared diseases of our day. It is the second leading cause of death, second only to heart disease. Often when a patient is diagnosed with cancer, there doesn't seem to be any apparent reason. There are so many different types of cancer. Some cancers are hereditary. Some cancers are linked to chemicals we breathe or with which we come in contact. Unfortunately, there is no cure. The cancer can be removed if caught early enough, or if properly treated, it can lie dormant in remission. Our bodies are made up of cells. Scientists have concluded that the average body contains 37.2 trillion cells and have 200 different types. Cancer has been described as a "cell gone bad." On the Cancer Treatment Centers of America website, I was reading a blog entitled "Cancer: When good cells go bad." The blog stated,

> Cells form our muscles and our bones. They help us turn food and oxygen into energy. They heal our wounds and keep us well. Like good soldiers, cells perform their vital duties with strict protocols and in amazing order. They communicate and cooperate with cells around them. Then, when they have given their all, they kill themselves to make room for new, healthy cells.

Bad cells abandon these rules. The bad cell divides uncontrollably and produces too many cells, resulting in a tumor. In a comparison used in this same blog, the writer adds,

> Normal cells know when to stop growing; cancer cells grow with abandon with no regard to the space around them. Normal cells kill themselves when their duties are done. A process called apoptosis; cancer cells ignore signals to die and, without treatment, may divide indefinitely and become virtually immortal. Normal cells communicate to help their host survive and thrive; cancer cells communicate only to deceive the body's defenses.[4]

Simply put, cancer cells don't obey the rules. They are self-centered and deceitful as they spread throughout the body. By neglecting the rules, they do things in their own way. If cancer is left unattended, it will most likely cause death to the body. Cancer must be dealt with sooner rather than later and the sooner the better. The church body also can be destroyed by cancerous members. The members are like cells working in unity. Reproducing by spreading the gospel, they grow and work for the good of the body for the glory of our Savior Jesus Christ; but then there is that one bad cell, or member, who turns out to be self-centered. He doesn't obey the rules and deceives himself and others. He does things to consume things for his own lust. That one will bring discouragement and resentment by sowing discord among the brethren, which, according to Proverbs 6:16–19, is an abomination to the Lord.

When the work of the cell is complete, it kills itself to make room for the younger healthier cells. I'm certainly not saying to kill ourselves, but sometimes it is best to step back if one is no longer able to perform as they once did. Understand, we are not to retire from the things of

---

4 "Cancer: When good cells go bad," *Cancer Treatment Center of America,* by CTCA; August 24, 2016.

the Lord, we should always have a part, but when a person has become more of a hindrance, which can cause a cancer in the church, they should step back and let the younger, more able Christians take the reins. It is important to train the younger generation since they are our future. Train them, then trust and support them. Of course, always be that mentor to whom they can come at any time.

The cancer must be removed. You've heard the old saying, "One bad apple spoils the bunch." If one apple is rotten, remove that apple or the rot will spread through the good apples. Church discipline is necessary, but it is one of the most difficult things with which a church has to deal. It can cause pain and hurt feelings to many close members. When the surgeon removes the cancer from the patient, he does it very carefully with precision, making sure not to harm other parts of the body. Church discipline is to be done in love not only to protect the body, but also to restore that member of the body. Jesus says,

> Moreover if thy brother shall trespass against thee, go and tell him his fault between thee and him alone: if he shall hear thee, thou hast gained thy brother. But if he will not hear thee, then take with thee one or two more, that in the mouth of two or three witnesses every word may be established. And if he shall neglect to hear them, tell it unto the church: but if he neglect to hear the church, let him be unto thee as an heathen man and a publican. (Matt. 18:15–17)

When that one cell in the church begins to go bad, we are to go in private not to embarrass or cause harm. It is in no way an attempt to destroy someone's reputation or character. The issue may be just a simple misunderstanding. If we only knew how many times we have offended someone and didn't even realize it, meaning no harm. After we go to that one and nothing is resolved, bring a few witnesses, again in love, seeking to restore the member. Finally, if nothing is resolved, it needs to go before the church, again only in love; and if nothing is resolved, then the member needs to no longer be a member of that church and the Lord shall deal with him as He sees fit. If things are left alone and not resolved, division will begin, and strife will be in the hearts of the members, thereby quenching the work of the Holy Spirit within the church. Also, with sin in the church, the outward appearance will begin to change, and the church will seem unhealthy to the community and no longer be the testimony it needs to be to win souls for the Lord.

I am reminded of a dear friend who was in church one day, when a concerned member went to him and said, "Your color doesn't look good. You should see a doctor." After a few tests, he was diagnosed with prostate cancer, and it had spread to his lymph nodes. What was going on inside changed the appearance of the outside. Many of our churches today are no longer inviting to those people on the outside. The church should be a place of learning and a place of love and comradery, not a place of fighting and strife. James tells us in James 4:1, "From whence come wars and fightings among you? Come they not hence, even of your lusts that war in your members?" We fight because we lust. We desire for our own personal gain rather than what is best to glorify God. We are servants of ourselves, not of Christ; and I'm afraid that, as churches today, our color doesn't look good.

As we said earlier, Satan has sought to destroy everything the Lord has created, the church especially. In the early church, many people heard the gospel and believed and were added to the church. As the church grew, opposition also grew. Persecution came against the believers, but Jesus promised in Matthew 16:18, "And I say also unto thee, That thou art Peter, and upon this rock I will build my church; and the gates of hell shall not prevail against it." Jesus would build the church upon Himself, and not even death or Satan could overcome or destroy it. Although Satan cannot destroy the church, that doesn't keep him from trying. He persecuted the early church from the outside. The people fled to other parts of the world for safety but continued to spread the gospel, so rather than Satan destroying the church, he helped spread the church throughout the world making it even greater. Satan still seeks to destroy the church from the outside, but has far greater success on the inside. He can take a little pride, a little jealousy, a little hatred and bitterness and rip a local church wide open. We need to "trust the Lord," "lean not to our own understanding," depend on Christ in our lives, and, in love, seek to serve Christ and others in the church for His name's sake. If one depends on himself and turns to his own desires, he becomes one as James describes:

> But every man is tempted, when he is drawn away of his own lust, and enticed. Then when lust hath conceived, it bringeth forth sin: and sin, when it is finished, bringeth forth death. (James 1:14–15)

Lust is the cancer not dealt with, which brings sin and then death.

Sin is a slippery slope. It will take you farther than you want to go and keep you far longer than you would ever want to stay. Just move a little from the Lord and seek the things of the world for just a season, and you have become a cancerous cell before you know it. Most churches are divided over little things that don't even matter. It could be someone just had a little too much pride to say "I'm sorry" or would prefer to gossip and talk behind someone's back rather than to go to that one in love. Before you know it, the camps are divided. The football team gels in the preseason coming together as brothers to work together for a common goal, but I have seen teams that are made up of players with egos. Those players seek their own glory; and when things don't go their way, they begin to look down on the others and are casting blame, pointing the finger instead of encouraging, stepping up to help, and working a little harder. Before it is realized, the cancer has grown within the team; and as the schedule gets tougher, the team will certainly fail, no matter how talented the team. The church is no different. It will likewise not be successful.

The United States of America is the strongest nation on earth. Any enemy that attempts to destroy us cannot succeed if they attack from the outside. Looking back in history, this nation was founded on biblical principles. The constitution was based on the Holy Bible. The Word of God was not only the foundation of this nation but also the foundation of the families who built the nation. The founders may not have all been Christians, but they reverenced and respected the Word of God. As time has gone on, the Word of God and respect for it are no longer taught in the homes; therefore, the homes are left in tatters. Just stop and look around. With the destruction of the homes comes the destruction of the churches. When children are not taught at home, they don't make it to the churches. Church doesn't mean anything; it's not important to them.

I love sports as much as the next guy, so I'm certainly not against organized sports. In fact, I think they can teach kids many important life lessons. But sports have taken the place of church and learning the Word of God. It's more important to spend our Sundays playing ball. Every parent wants their kid to be the star of the show, get a full scholarship, and maybe go pro. Wake-up call! Few athletes ever make it that far. Christians may earn a scholarship to a liberal college, but they are soon brainwashed. They are taught there is no God and that the morals about which their parents told them don't matter. Many other interests have taken the place of the church, and before long, we have raised a generation that knows not the Lord, a generation like the one found in the book of Joshua. This rising younger generation no longer has morals. These young people are no longer accountable to God. They don't believe in God. In schools, they are taught they are animals, so why would you expect any different? It's not long until the nation accepts things it once rejected and it is deceived into thinking government and government programs are the answer. Whatever makes me feel good goes. The family has been destroyed, the church is in ruins, and the nation has soon lost its freedom. It was once a team of united citizens that became the United States. Now the views are so different. We and our leaders are so divided. There will never be unity without an old-fashioned revival. Jesus tells us in Matthew 12:25, "Every Kingdom divided against itself is brought to desolation; and every city or house divided against itself shall not stand." This nation will probably not be destroyed from the outside, but from the inside and the cancer with which it never dealt.

Maddie continues to point. Waiting, she depends on me to make the next move. I quickly swing around in front of her. Maddie's eyes look at me and then at the bird without ever moving her head. It's as if she is saying, "There it is, Chris. I have done my part. Don't screw it up." Suddenly with the sound of thundering wings, the bird flies. I quickly react with the gun to my shoulder. I swing the gun in front of the bird, and with the squeeze of the trigger, the explosion echoes though the woods. The grouse falls to the ground. Before I can say a word, Maddie bounds through the brush, grabs the bird in her mouth, and brings it back to me. I grab her around the neck and praise her, "Good job, Maddie Ol' Girl!" Looking at Maddie and seeing the success of working as a team reminds me that, as Christians, we are just pilgrims passing through on a long journey. I see it's not so much the journey but those we meet along the way and those relationships and bonds we form as we unite to accomplish the common goal of serving and seeking to glorify our Lord and Savior Jesus Christ. We cherish and thank the Lord each day for the privilege of experiencing the comradery.

COMING HOME

The shadows begin to grow longer as we head back toward the truck. The air becomes cool and crisp with a little bite. The sun is now covered by a few dark clouds. The mountains seem to be on fire with an explosion of red and orange. As the day comes to a close, they turn a dark purple. The great symphony dies down. The birds are no longer chirping, the squirrels have returned to their nests, and even the sound of the few katydids has diminished. Below, I can still hear the trickle of the small stream. Above, I hear the whistle of the wings as two wood ducks, headed to roost, fly over. The day is almost done, and night is setting in.

The sun appears to be only a few feet from the top of the mountain range. I am amazed at how fast the earth moves. Time really does fly, but you don't realize it until the last few minutes of the day. It's as if I can see the sun moving, and then before I know it, the sun has disappeared. James gives us a good example in James 4:14: "Whereas ye know not what shall be on the morrow. For what is your life? It is even a vapour that appeareth for a little time, and then vanisheth away."

Life may seem long; however, in the scope of eternity it is but a vapor. When the sun is at its peak, it seems like we have an eternity to do the things we want, but as the day comes to an end, we realize that time is short. Our lives likewise seem so long. It appears as if we have so much time, but before we know it, the sun will set on our lives here on this earth. I once heard a story of a preacher who was fifty years old, and was finishing Bible college. He went to his professor and asked, "Should I continue advancing my education, or should I start preaching?" The professor thought a second and replied, "You're fifty years old. You have wasted enough time. Get to work." Life is short, only a vapor. Life will come to an end.

Over time, these old bodies wear out. They are susceptible to disease and other physical and mental problems. There comes a time in our lives when we can no longer carry on. We become tired. We see it in many elderly people and terminally ill patients. We pray that the Lord would somehow see fit to heal them so they can continue on with a full life, but it's not always the Lord's will. It's time for Him to take them through the doorway of death. So why do we have to die? Why can't we just live here forever? Why does the day have to come to an end?

After the sin of Adam and Eve in the Garden of Eden, God cursed the earth and man. He told Adam that he was made from dust and therefore he would return to that same dust because of his sin. Man now had a sin nature, a wicked heart to do his own desires. Since Adam and Eve were the first two people on earth, every person would then have to descend from them, and each descendant would have that very sin nature. In the midst of the Garden of Eden was the tree of life. If Adam and Eve had eaten of that tree, they would have lived forever, in a wicked sinful, cursed state. God didn't want to see His creation live in that cursed state for eternity. He loved mankind, so He cast them out of the garden, never to return again. Man must die in order to separate from this sinful, cursed body. Imagine living forever with cancer and other diseases or in this world of corruption, wickedness, sorrow, and pain with no exit. For that reason, man had to die. Hebrews 9:27 tells us, "And as it is appointed unto men once to die, but after this the judgment." It is obvious that at some point and time each one of us will die. God says He created man from the dust of the earth and breathed the breath of life into him and made him a living soul. When a child is born, he progresses to a certain age and then regresses until the death of the body, which decays. Man turns back to the dust from which he came, back to where he began, just as God said.

Creation is in the state of wickedness and suffering. Death is inevitable, and there is a desire for change. Paul tells us in Romans 8:18–23,

> For I reckon that the sufferings of this present time are not worthy to be compared with the glory which shall be revealed in us. For the earnest expectation of the creature waiteth for the manifestation of the sons of God. For the creature was made subject to vanity, not willingly, but by reason of him who hath subjected the same in hope, Because the creature itself also shall be delivered from the bondage of corruption into the glorious liberty of the children of God. For we know that the whole creation groaneth and travaileth in pain together until now. And not only they, but ourselves also, which have the firstfruits of the Spirit, even we ourselves groan within ourselves, waiting for the adoption, to wit, the redemption of our body.

Throughout history man has sought to make the world a perfect place but has failed. No matter how hard man tries, through education, religion, social programs, and even peace talks, wars continue to be fought and murderers still roam the streets. Man's idea of peace will always end with corruption because of man's wicked heart. Man has sought a cure for all the diseases and pestilences that we face. Although he has found many cures and solutions for medical issues, he has never found a cure for everything. We still age and deteriorate, we still face disease, and we still die. There will never be peace, and there will always be sickness and death on earth until the Lord comes to set up His kingdom; therefore, all creation groans and travails in pain, waiting to leave these cursed bodies and this cursed earth.

Our desire is to be in perfection where everything is perfect, a place where our bodies are perfect as well as the atmosphere in which we live; a place where there is no more pain and suffering, no more tears and no more death. As we seek perfection, God is perfect and is in perfection; and yes, God desires that we live in perfection with Him for all eternity, which is why He made a way of salvation for us through His perfect son Jesus Christ. Since God is perfect, we must be perfect in order to be in His presence. God is eternal, and we also need to be eternal. We cannot stand in the presence of God in these filthy, sinful bodies. We cannot dwell with God for eternity in a body that is only temporary. That is the reason Paul tells us in 1 Corinthians 15:53, "For this corruptible must put on incorruption, and this mortal must put on immortality." God so loved you and me that He sent his perfect son to die on the cross for every sin that has ever been committed and that ever will be committed. He was that perfect sacrifice. When we believe and receive Him as our Savior, we are born again. Then we are promised glorified bodies that are covered with the perfect righteousness of Jesus Christ, allowing us to stand before a perfect and Holy God, and a body that will never die but will live with Him in perfection for all eternity when we leave this earth. I am reminded of the words of Paul: "To be absent from the body is to be present with the Lord" and "For me to live is Christ, to die is gain."

With a grouse in the bag and a few flushes, Maddie and I had a pretty good day. It's late, and I'm getting tired and hungry. I look forward to going home. Rebecca will be there waiting for me when I walk through the door. As always, I will give her a hug and a big kiss on the lips. Knowing Rebecca and how she loves to cook, I know she will have a nice meal ready for me when I get there. There will be a fire in the fireplace. Maddie will curl up on her bed and probably not move until the morning. Rebecca and I will sit around and enjoy each other's company over a hot cup of coffee. I will tell her some of the things that happened today and make up a few stories that didn't. It's like the fish—the big one always gets away. I have learned over the years that though it's always nice to get out and hunt, there is nothing like coming home.

I once heard a man say that preachers spend a lot of time teaching how to live but rarely about how to die. I'm not talking about the physical act of death but the expectation, the joy of going home.

When one comes to the end of life, there is that fear of the unknown. Yes, there are many things we won't know until we get there, but the Bible tells us many things that we can know and that can be comforting to us as we go through our daily walk of life.

Billy Graham once said, "Death is not the end of life. It is only the gateway to eternity." Death is stepping out into eternity. We have never been there, so of course, it can be a fearful event. At a news conference Billy Graham was asked if he was afraid of dying. He replied, "No, I look forward to it with great anticipation." How could one be so confident? Billy Graham had a relationship with Jesus Christ. He spent time in the scriptures studying so that he would know what to expect and could look forward to the great expectation.

Do you know what to expect when you go through the doorway of death? You can know just as well as Mr. Graham, but it begins with a relationship with Jesus Christ. Do you know Him as your Savior? Have you believed and accepted His gift of the work on Calvary's cross? If you have, you are a child of God, and your Father in heaven will give you the same knowledge He gave Billy Graham through the Holy Spirit, if you seek those things in your life. The Lord wants us to have knowledge of what is to come. Paul used the phrase many times: "I would not have you to be ignorant, brethren." Jesus tells us in John 15:15,

> Henceforth I call you not servants; for the servant knoweth not what his lord doeth: but I have called you friends; for all things that I have heard of my Father I have made known unto you.

He wants us to not only have knowledge of the things to come but also not to fear those things. John used the phrase "That your joy may be full." How can we be joyful while living in fear? Jesus used the phrase "Fear not" to his disciples any time they were afraid. Although death, future wars, judgments, hell, and the wrath of God can be fearful things, I want to share with you just a basic view of what the Word of God has to say about these events and the things to come, not that you should fear but that you may look forward with great anticipation and that your joy may be full.

Jesus told his disciples He was going away to prepare a place for them and when He went away He would come back to receive them. I can only imagine what it will be like. The beauty that surrounds me as I walk through these mountains cannot compare to what we will experience in heaven. During the ministry of our Lord, Jesus spoke more about hell than heaven. Why? Because Jesus came to warn man that he was a sinner and on his way to hell, a Christ-less eternity, and mankind needed a Savior. Jesus brought the good news of the gospel message: "For God so loved the world, that he gave his only begotten Son, that whosoever believeth in him should not perish, but have everlasting life" (John 3:16). Jesus said, "I love you and I want you to spend eternity with me in heaven, not in the place that I created for Satan and his angels, that place called Hell, where you will be tormented with burning fire forever and ever." Also, I believe Jesus didn't speak as much about heaven because He didn't want believers to focus so much on the finish line that they neglect to run the race.

In 1993, I ran in the Marine Corps Marathon in Washington, DC. I was just an average runner. I set a goal of four hours or less and finished in around the 3:50s. I started training late, so the most I ever ran previously at one time was eighteen miles. I felt pretty good until around mile twenty. At that point, my feet began to feel like boards, my knees and ankles were hurting, and I was getting tired. To motivate myself, I thought of the finish line. Just like in life, it's good to know where the finish line is, but it can be overwhelming if you focus on that rather than the course. I looked down at my feet, and I thought, *Just put one foot in front of the other.* Around mile twenty-four, people began to line the streets, perfect strangers whom I had never met. They were cheering us on, clapping and encouraging. Off in the distance, I could hear the marching band. Adrenaline began to kick in, and my body was becoming numb to the pain. The pace began to increase, and I knew I was getting close. Finally, at mile twenty-six and two more tenths, I crossed the finish line. Someone grabbed me, wrapped a solar blanket around me, and said, "Great job!" They later placed a medal around my neck and rewarded me for finishing the race.

Life is a long grueling marathon. There will be pain and suffering, and there will be many times we have to look down and say, "Just put one foot in front of the other." Thank the Lord for those along the way who encourage and cheer us on. We are also encouraged by the promises of God from His Word; and though we can't see the finish line, we know when we put our faith and trust in Him, that it is not too far ahead. Then without warning, whether through death or through the rapture, we will cross that finish line; and Jesus Christ our Lord will wrap us in a white robe of righteousness and say, "Well done, thou good and faithful servant," and later reward us with a crown of glory. We are reminded in 1 Corinthians 13:12, "For now we see through a glass, darkly; but then face to face: now I know in part; but then shall I know even as also I am known." As Paul tells us, we can only get a glimpse. We don't know all about our Lord and what to expect, but when we see Him face-to-face, we will know as we know ourselves.

Have you ever wondered what it's going to be like as we walk through those pearly gates of heaven? I wonder if just like the marathon. Friends and family will be there cheering us on as we cross the finish line. Imagine parents, grandparents, brothers or sisters, even children who went on before us and had trusted Jesus as Savior. Of course, nothing will be greater than to see our Savior, the one who loved us so much He willingly suffered for us and died in our place on the cross, and finally meet Him face-to-face. Jesus will be there to greet us. Wow! What comfort and joy we face as Christians! There are many differing opinions of what He might look like. There have been many paintings of Him. I don't know, but I just want to share some verses of how the Bible describes our Lord. After the resurrection of our Lord Jesus Christ, He appeared to His disciples. Paul writes in 1 Corinthians 15:5–6,

> And that he was seen of Cephas, then of the twelve: After that, he was seen of above five hundred brethren at once; of whom the greater part remain unto this present, but some are fallen asleep.

Jesus was seen by them before His ascension. He must have looked as He did before the crucifixion, with the exception that now he had scars, because everyone recognized Him as Jesus.

About sixty years later, when John was on the island of Patmos, he had a vision. This was the time when he wrote the book of Revelation, or the Revelation of Jesus Christ. The word *Revelation* simply means "to reveal," so we can word it "The revealing of Jesus Christ." John heard a voice saying, "I am the Alpha and Omega, the first and the last." The voice commanded him to write and send this message to the seven churches, and as he turns to see who is speaking, he sees Jesus, "the one who loved him." He tells us in Revelation 1:12–16,

> And I turned to see the voice that spake with me. And being turned, I saw seven golden candlesticks; and in the midst of the seven candlesticks one like unto the Son of man, clothed with a garment down to the foot, and girt about the paps with a golden girdle. His head and his hairs were white like wool, as white as snow; and his eyes were as a flame of fire; and his feet like unto fine brass, as if they burned in a furnace; and his voice as the sound of many waters. And he had in his right hand seven stars: and out of his mouth went a sharp two-edged sword: and his countenance was as the sun shineth in his strength.

Jesus was clothed in pure white, picturing His purity; the gold, His deity; and the brass, His suffering and sacrifice for our sins. His tongue was as the Word of God, a two-edged sword; His eyes as fire lighting up the darkness (nothing can be hidden as He judges the world); and His countenance or His complexion as bright as the sun. Notice a few other verses throughout the Bible. Moses was in the presence of the Lord for forty days and forty nights on Mount Sinai, where he was receiving the Law of the Lord. When he returned, his appearance had changed. We pick this up in Exodus 34:29–30.

> And it came to pass, when Moses came down from mount Sinai with the two tables of testimony in Moses' hand, when he came down from the mount, that Moses wist not that the skin of his face shone while he talked with him. And when Aaron and all the children of Israel saw Moses, behold, the skin of his face shone; and they were afraid to come nigh him.

The face of Moses reflected the glory of God as he spent time in His presence. During His earthly ministry, Jesus went up into the mount for what we call the transfiguration, in which His appearance was changed.

> And after six days Jesus taketh Peter, James, and John his brother, and bringeth them up into an high mountain apart, and was transfigured before them: and his face did shine as the sun, and his raiment was white as the light. (Matt. 17:1–2)

Notice the common appearance each time one is in the presence of God: their complexion changes, they shine and they glow. If you have trusted Jesus Christ as your Savior and spend time with God in his Word and in fellowship, then you should be different. You should have a glow. Your countenance should reflect the light that is burning within you by the Holy Spirit. As Jesus was transfigured, He was changed. It was a picture of what John saw in the book of Revelation. It is also what we will see when we see Jesus. He will be as bright as the sun. It is also a picture of what we, as Christians, will look like when we are changed in that moment into our new glorified bodies. "Beloved, now are we the sons of God, and it doth not yet appear what we shall be: but we know that, when he shall appear, we shall be like him; for we shall see him as he is" (1 John 3:2).

There will come a day, and I believe it to be soon, in which the church will be raptured out of this world.

> But I would not have you to be ignorant, brethren, concerning them which are asleep, that ye sorrow not, even as others which have no hope. For if we believe that Jesus died and rose again, even so them also which sleep in Jesus will God bring with him. For this we say unto you by the word of the Lord, that we which are alive and remain unto the coming of the Lord shall not prevent them which are asleep. For the Lord himself shall descend from heaven with a shout, with the voice of the archangel, and with the trump of God: and the dead in Christ shall rise first: Then we which are alive and remain shall be caught up together with them in the clouds, to meet the Lord in the air: and so shall we ever be with the Lord. Wherefore comfort one another with these words. (1 Thess. 4:13–18)

The Bible mentions two resurrections. The first resurrection has phases. The first phase of the first resurrection was when Jesus Christ arose from the grave on the third day after His crucifixion; the second phase will be when he raptures the church. The word *rapture* means "to snatch out." In a moment, in a twinkling of an eye, which is faster than the blink of an eye, the Lord will come; and the dead, those who have been saved and passed on, will be changed. Think about your loved ones who have gone on before you. Their dead bodies are decaying in the grave. The Bible says they will be reunited with their bodies, but their bodies will be changed to glorified bodies, incorruptible and immortal. Then we who are still alive will be changed as well and have glorified bodies that will never die, bodies that can stand before God and last for all eternity. There we shall ever be with the Lord. Hallelujah. Amen. The rapture is the next event on God's calendar. No man knows the time or the day. He could come at any time. Are you ready? Have you trusted Jesus as your Savior today?

After the rapture, Christians will be judged for their works. Many people believe that at the end of time, there will be one judgment, when we will all stand before God and He will judge our good works and our bad. If our good outweighs the bad, then we are in, and if the bad outweighs the good, we will be punished for all eternity. This belief is false. As we have seen, there are two resurrections, but we will also see more than one judgment. The first phase of the first resurrection was Jesus Christ arising from the grave, the second phase is the rapture of the church, and the third phase comes after the tribulation. These again are all part of the first resurrection.

> Blessed and holy is he that hath part in the first resurrection: on such the second death hath no power, but they shall be priests of God and of Christ, and shall reign with him a thousand years. (Rev. 20:6)

These people are all who have trusted Jesus Christ as Savior. We will all reign with Him in his kingdom for one thousand years. The first judgment came before the first resurrection, when Jesus, that perfect Lamb, hung on the cross, taking upon Himself the sins of the world. With all the sin of the world on His son, God turned His back because He could not look on sin. Therefore, darkness covered the earth that day. Think of it like this: the time was at hand; God had enough; and He was going to judge the world for sin, every sin that was ever committed or ever will be. God was requiring judgment, and He was going to destroy all mankind and send us all to the lake of fire. Because man is a sinner, this judgment is what man deserves "for the wages of sin is death." But because of God's love, He gave his only Son, the perfect sinless Lamb, as the substitute, taking our sins upon Himself and paying the price with His precious blood. God judged our sins by the blood of His Son. That was the first judgment. On the third day, He arose again as the first phase of the first resurrection. All who believe and accept his payment will be saved, or born again.

The second judgment is for the believer. As we go through our daily walks, we will not be perfect, we will fall short, and we will sin against our loving God. When we sin, the Holy Spirit convicts us of our sin, and we are to repent and confess it to God. "If we confess our sins, he is faithful and just to forgive us our sins, and to cleanse us from all unrighteousness" (1 John 1:9). In this self-judgment, we judge ourselves. When the Holy Spirit convicts us of our sins, we are to judge, repent, and ask for forgiveness.

The third judgment occurs at the bema seat of Christ, also known as the judgment seat of Christ. That judgment, coming after the rapture (the second phase of the first resurrection), will take place in heaven. All who have believed and accepted Jesus Christ as Savior will stand before Him in judgment. This is not a judgment for the sins that we committed, because our sins were judged and paid for on the cross in the first judgment. When you receive Jesus, you have accepted His payment; therefore, your sins are forgiven and forgotten. As David said in Psalm 103:12, "As far as the east is from the west, so far hath he removed our transgressions from us." This is a judgment of our works, a time of rewards. God knows our hearts and motives for everything we do, and on that day, we will be judged by how we spent our time and what we accomplished on earth. We get more insight in 1 Corinthians 3:12–15:

> Now if any man build upon this foundation gold, silver, precious stones, wood, hay, stubble; every man's work shall be made manifest: for the day shall declare it, because it shall be revealed by fire; and the fire shall try every man's work of what sort it is. If any man's work abide which he hath built thereupon, he shall receive a reward. If any man's work shall be burned, he shall suffer loss: but he himself shall be saved; yet so as by fire.

If we spend our lives looking for the next dollar or seeking to fulfill our own lust and personal gain, those works are wood, hay, and stubble that will burn up and leave us empty-handed. If we seek first the kingdom of God and His righteousness and spend our time serving Christ, then our works are as silver and gold, which will stand through the fire. At this judgment, we will be rewarded for our earthly accomplishments. Paul, being a Roman citizen, enjoyed the Olympics, especially running. He used the analogy of running a race to explain the rewards.

> Know ye not that they which run in a race run all, but one receiveth the prize? So run, that ye may obtain. And every man that striveth for the mastery is temperate in all things. Now they do it to obtain a corruptible crown; but we and incorruptible. (1 Cor. 9:24–25)

Anything we receive in this life will eventually be destroyed. When I finished the Marine Corps Marathon, I was rewarded a medal for finishing the race; but that medal can be lost, stolen, or even destroyed. The medal is temperate, or corruptible. In the ancient Olympic Games, the winner received a *kotinos*, a wreath made from a wild olive branch. Over time the leaves would wither; and the crown, which was a corruptible crown, would fade away. The rewards we will receive in heaven from our Lord Jesus Christ will be incorruptible.

The Bible speaks of five crowns that will be rewarded to the saints at this time. The first is the incorruptible crown that was just mentioned. Paul goes on to say in 1 Corinthians 9:26–27,

> I therefore so run, not as uncertainly; so fight I, not as one that beateth the air: But I keep under my body, and bring it into subjection: lest that by any means, when I have preached to others, I myself should be a castaway.

This incorruptible crown is the victor's crown, a reward for keeping our bodies under subjection and not yielding to the lusts of the flesh. We accomplish those things by keeping Christ in the center of our lives and allowing the Holy Spirit to direct our paths.

The second crown is the crown of righteousness. Paul speaks of this crown in 2 Timothy 4:6–8:

> For I am now ready to be offered, and the time of my departure is at hand. I have fought a good fight, I have finished my course, I have kept the faith: Henceforth there is laid up for me a crown of righteousness, which the Lord, the righteous judge, shall give me at that day: and not to me only, but unto all them also that love his appearing.

Paul's life was coming to an end. He would soon face death by being beheaded, but Paul wasn't concerned with the suffering in this world. He longed to see Jesus face-to-face. Not only will Paul receive this crown, but also all who look forward to the coming of our Savior, continue to live for Him, and keep our bodies under subjection.

The third crown is the crown of rejoicing, also known as the soul winner's crown. Paul tells us in 1 Thessalonians 2:19–20, "For what is our hope, or joy, or crown of rejoicing? Are not even ye in the presence of our Lord Jesus Christ at his coming? For ye are our glory and joy." Paul, one of the greatest missionaries in history, lived for Christ. He was willingly beaten, arrested, thrown into prison, and eventually beheaded. For what? That people might hear the good news of the gospel and be saved! As he wrote to the church in Thessalonica, he rejoiced knowing that because of his work they also would be in the presence of God. They were his glory and joy. Just think, you and I today have that same opportunity to present the gospel of Jesus Christ so others might be saved. We can rejoice knowing they will be with us in heaven and we will receive that crown of rejoicing.

The fourth crown is the crown of glory, the elder's or pastor's crown. Peter writes about this crown.

> The elders which are among you I exhort, who am also an elder, and a witness of the sufferings of Christ, and also a partaker of the glory that shall be revealed: Feed the flock of God which is among you, taking the oversight thereof, not by constraint, but willingly; not for filthy lucre, but of a ready mind; Neither as being lords over God's heritage, but being ensamples to the flock. And when the chief Shepherd shall appear, ye shall receive a crown of glory that fadeth not away. (1 Pet. 5:1–4)

God doesn't call all men to pastor when they are saved, but it is a marvelous privilege for those men he calls. Some men have rejected the call. Others have disqualified themselves and cannot answer the call. Some preachers were never called and have no business in that position, but there are those men who preach not for personal gain but for the glory of God. They have a heart for the flock and a desire to see souls saved and saints edified, or lifted up. I have said many times that "A preacher preaches to live, but a pastor lives to preach." The position of a pastor is for life, twenty-four hours a day, seven days a week, with a heart of a bird dog. When pastors stand before Jesus, the Master, as a true servant, they will receive the crown of glory.

Finally, we have the crown of life. Also known as the martyrs' crown, it is mentioned in two separate passages by James and also by John in the book of Revelation. "Blessed is the man that endureth temptation: for when he is tried, he shall receive the crown of life, which the Lord hath promised to them that love him" (James 1:12). John writes in Revelation 2:10,

> Fear none of those things which thou shalt suffer: behold, the devil shall cast some of you

into prison, that ye may be tried; and ye shall
have tribulation ten days: be thou faithful unto
death, and I will give thee a crown of life.

As Jesus taught the disciples, he warned that they would be hated
by the world, because the world first hated Jesus, and they would be
persecuted for His name's sake. Jesus Christ is a threat to man's lifestyle. He was then, and He is now. Everyone who carries the gospel is a
threat to the world, but when people hear the gospel and believe in the
Lord Jesus Christ as Savior, He becomes a blessing. The one who was
once to them a divider is now to them a uniter. Throughout the history of the church, men and women have been persecuted and killed
for the cause of Christ. They have been tortured, burned at the stake,
beheaded, and taken by many other means of brutal death. Today we
have peace in America, although in other parts of the world, it is not
so peaceful. Christians are still being killed, and it's only a matter of
time before it happens here. In the tribulation period, the people who
reject the mark of the beast will be killed. I believe we will begin to
see these events before the church is raptured, worldwide. But don't
be afraid. Be faithful unto death and rejoice because blessed is that
man who endureth temptation for Jesus will reward you a crown of
life. Christians have so much for which to look forward. Our sins are
behind us. Our rewards are before us. Upon receiving our crowns, we
will give glory and praise to our savior. Realizing that without Christ
we would never achieve these rewards, in humble adoration, we will
cast our crowns at the feet of our Savior, giving Him praise honor and
glory. Revelation 4:10–11 says,

> The four and twenty elders fall down before
> him that sat on the throne, and worship him that
> liveth for ever and ever, and cast their crowns
> before the throne, saying, Thou art worthy, O
> Lord, to receive glory and honour and power: for
> thou hast created all things, and for thy pleasure
> they are and were created.

After this judgment, there will come a great event for each believer. In our younger days, we look forward to the day when we will marry the man or woman of our dreams, our princess or prince charming. I remember the day when I stood at the front of the church awaiting my bride, the most beautiful woman in the world, the one I adore, my best friend, and the one with whom I want to spend the rest of my life. Before God and man, I promised to love and be faithful to her no matter the circumstance. Jesus, who is called faithful and true, awaits His beautiful bride, the church. We are told by Paul in Ephesians 5:25–27,

> Husbands, love your wives, even as Christ also loved the church, and gave himself for it; That he might sanctify and cleanse it with the washing of water by the word, That he might present it to himself a glorious church, not having spot, or wrinkle, or any such thing; but that it should be holy and without blemish.

My father-in-law walked Rebecca down the aisle of the church. She was adorned in a beautiful white dress as he presented her to me. At this time, the church will be presented to Christ as His bride. We will be dressed in pure white as a symbol of perfection. Isaiah tells us, "Come now, and let us reason together, saith the LORD: though your sins be as scarlet, they shall be as white as snow; though they be red like crimson, they shall be as wool" (Isaiah 1:18). As the bride of Christ, we have Christ's righteousness. He has washed us as white as snow. Paul goes on to say in Ephesians 5:32, "This is a great mystery: but I speak concerning Christ and the church."

In biblical times it was Jewish tradition that a man would be espoused to his bride, similar to our engagements today, only more of a binding contract. Often the bride would be bought with a price. After the purchase, the bridegroom would then return to prepare a place for his new bride. Before the wedding, the bridegroom with the wedding party would leave his father's house and go to the bride's house, where she would be anxiously waiting. The bridegroom would take her and bring her to either his house or his father's house, and there would be a great wedding party full of singing and dancing. It would be a joyous occasion with family and friends. Jesus came to earth to die on the cross and pay the price for the sins of the world, to espouse his bride, "all who believe." He then went to His Father's house to prepare a place as He promised in John 14:1–3. One day He is going to return for His bride, the church. We anxiously wait for Him to take us back to His Father's house, where there will be singing and joy unspeakable such as we have never seen. John writes in Revelation 19:6–8,

> And I heard as it were the voice of a great multitude, and as the voice of many waters, and as the voice of mighty thunderings, saying, Alleluia: for the Lord God omnipotent reigneth. Let us be glad, and rejoice, and give honor to him: for the marriage of the Lamb is come, and his wife hath made herself ready. And to her was granted that she should be arrayed in fine linen, clean and white: for the fine linen is the righteousness of saints.

What a beautiful picture of what is to come for the believer! We will be presented pure and perfect to our Lord and Savior Jesus Christ at the great wedding supper.

While we are being rewarded at the judgment seat of Christ and during the marriage supper in heaven, there will be a far different scene here on earth. The great tribulation, when God pours out his judgment and wrath on earth, will occur. It will be a time of famine, devastation, and death. Many people will be deceived and receive the mark of the beast, and they will be doomed for eternity. Midway through this awful time, 144,000 Jews will believe on the Lord Jesus Christ and be saved. They will then be the Lord's witnesses. The Antichrist will reject these Jews and attempt to destroy them. At the end of the seven-year period, Christ will return to destroy the enemies of these Jews in the great Battle of Armageddon. Of course, the marriage supper and the tribulation will end about the same time, because we, after the marriage supper, will follow Jesus as His army.

> And I saw heaven opened, and behold a
> white horse; and he that sat upon him was called
> Faithful and True, and in righteousness he doth
> judge and make war. His eyes were as a flame
> of fire, and on his head were many crowns; and
> he had a name written, that no man knew, but
> he himself. And he was clothed with a vesture
> dipped in blood: and his name is called The Word
> of God. And the armies which were in heaven
> followed him upon white horses, clothed in fine
> linen, white and clean. And out of his mouth
> goeth a sharp sword, that with it he should smite
> the nations: and he shall rule them with a rod of
> iron: and he treadeth the winepress of the fierce-
> ness and wrath of Almighty God. And he hath on
> his vesture and on his thigh a name written, KING
> OF KINGS, AND LORD OF LORDS. (Rev. 19:11–16)

This is the battle of Armageddon, when Jesus Christ our Lord will speak and blood will rise to the horses bridle.

At this time the Antichrist and the False Prophet will be cast into the lake of fire. Satan will then be bound and cast into the bottomless pit for one thousand years. The next judgment, the judgment of the nations, will begin.

All men still living at the end of the tribulation will stand before Jesus Christ, the Great Judge, here on earth for the judgment of the sheep and the goats. Jesus tells us of this great event in Matthew 25:31–34:

> When the Son of man shall, come in his glory,
> and all the holy angels with him, then shall he sit
> upon the throne of his glory: And before him shall
> be gathered all nations: and he shall separate them

one from another, as a shepherd divideth his sheep
from the goats: And he shall set the sheep on his
right hand, but the goats on the left. Then shall the
King say unto them on his right hand, Come, ye
blessed of my Father, inherit the kingdom prepared
for you from the foundation of the world.

During the tribulation, the Antichrist will attempt to destroy the
Jews. It will be much like the days of Hitler. Many of these Jews will
go into hiding. There will be few who will help them and take care of
them during this time. I am reminded of the old story of the "Hiding
Place." God is going to judge the nations. Those who helped will be
known as sheep. Those who didn't will be known as goats. Notice
Jesus said that these who help his people will inherit the kingdom.
Remember what Jesus said to Nicodemus in John 3:3, "Verily, verily, I
say unto the, Except a man be born again, he cannot see the kingdom
of God." In other words, something had to take place: they heard the
gospel of Jesus Christ and believed. They weren't saved by their works,
they were saved by faith, and their works were an action of their faith
in Jesus Christ. Those who reject the gospel and don't help will be
known as the goats. The Lord gives them their sentence in Matthew
25:41: "Then shall he say also unto them on the left hand, Depart
from me, ye cursed, into everlasting fire, prepared for the devil and his
angels." Verse 46 continues, "And these shall go away into everlasting
punishment: but the righteous into life eternal." At this time, Satan
is bound; the wicked are in everlasting fire; and Jesus Christ is on the
throne of David, where He will rule and reign for one thousand years.

During this time of peace on earth, all men will come and worship the King, and there will be no more war.

And he shall judge among the nations, and
shall rebuke many people: and they shall beat
their swords into plowshares, and their spears
into pruninghooks: nation shall not lift up sword
against nation, neither shall they learn war anymore. (Isa. 2:4)

Because of the presence of our Lord, there will be no more war. There will finally be peace in the Middle East, as man has tried to do so many times and failed. Christ will not only bring peace to man but also peace to the animal kingdom.

> The wolf also shall dwell with the lamb, and the leopard shall lie down with the kid; and the calf and the young lion and the fatling together; and a little child shall lead them. And the cow and the bear shall feed; their young ones shall lie down together: and the lion shall eat straw like the ox. And the sucking child shall play on the hole of the asp, and the weaned child shall put his hand on the cockatrice' den. They shall not hurt nor destroy in all my holy mountain: for the earth shall be full of the knowledge of the Lord, as the waters cover the sea. (Isa. 11:6–9)

During this one-thousand-year period, many children will be born. Though these sheep brought into the kingdom are born-again believers, they will still have the same sin nature we have today, and their children likewise will be born in sin. With the presence of the Lord and without the influence of Satan, they will make good citizens, and they will go every year to worship the King. If they don't, then the Lord will punish them by withholding the rain. At the end of the one thousand years, Satan will be released to deceive many of these people. Just like today, these people will have a choice to receive or reject Jesus as Savior. The people who reject Jesus as Savior will be deceived and join Satan one last time for battle, but the Lord will wipe them out.

At this time the second resurrection and the final judgment, the great white throne, will begin. Christians will not be judged since we are of the first resurrection. "Blessed and Holy is he that hath part in the first resurrection: on such the second death hath no power..." (Rev. 20:6). If you have trusted Jesus Christ as your Savior today, happy are you—you have much to look forward to. But if you reject the Savior, read Revelation 20:11–15.

> And I saw a great white throne, and him that sat on it, from whose face the earth and the heaven fled away; and there was found no place for them. And I saw the dead, small and great, stand before God; and the books were opened: and another book was opened, which is the book of life: and the dead were judged out of those things which were written in the books, according to their works. And the sea gave up the dead which were in it; and death and hell delivered up the dead which were in them: and they were judged every man according to their works. And death and hell were cast into the lake of fire. This is the second death. And whosoever was not found written in the book of life was cast into the lake of fire.

This day will be the most tragic day in human history. On this day, God will judge every person who has rejected Jesus Christ and His work on the cross. Those people will be judged for the sins they committed, all because they didn't accept the fact that Jesus paid for them all. They will spend eternity in torment. That is so tragic when the plan of salvation is so simple even a young child can understand. Jesus is calling! He paid the price on the cross. Won't you just come?

After the final judgment, all sinners and sin have been judged and wiped out completely. Earth will be destroyed by fire, and a new heaven and earth will be introduced. At this time, we hear the comforting words of Revelation 21:4:

> And God shall wipe away all tears from their eyes; and there shall be no more death, neither sorrow, nor crying, neither shall there be any more pain: for the former things are passed away.

God gives us a glimpse into the new heaven and new earth and, I believe, of what heaven is like today. It is a place that we on this earth can only imagine. The beauty will be unparalleled. Revelation 21:9–27 speaks of the great city as having the glory of God, being like a precious stone. John goes on to tell of the wall and the gates and give the dimensions. He describes the walls as jasper and the city as pure gold, so pure it is as glass. He names the twelve stones that garnished the wall: jasper, sapphire, chalcedony, emerald, sardonyx, sardius, chrysolite, beryl, topaz, chrysoprasus, jacinth, and amethyst. With the gates made of pearl and the streets of the city pure gold, we can only imagine the beauty, but that's not all verse 22 tells us. There is something missing. John saw no temple. "And I saw no temple therein: for the Lord God Almighty and the Lamb are the temple of it" (Rev. 21:22). In other words, we will dwell with God and our Savior the Lord Jesus Christ for eternity. Notice something else is different in this new heaven and earth. Remember when Moses was in God's presence and His face glowed? With God's glory, there is no need of light.

> And the city had no need of the sun, neither the moon, to shine in it: for the glory of God did lighten it, and the lamb is the light thereof. And the nations of them which are saved shall walk in the light of it: and the kings of the earth do bring their glory and honor into it. And the gates of it shall not be shut at all by day: for there shall be no night there. And they shall bring the glory and honor of the nations into it. (Rev. 21:23–26)

The Lord tells us of a place where there will be no night. With our glorified bodies, we will never tire so there will be no need of night. We will also dwell with our God face-to-face. And notice what comes out of his throne in Revelation 22:1–5:

> And he shewed me a pure river of water of life, clear as crystal, proceeding out of the throne of God and of the Lamb. In the midst of the

street of it, and on either side of the river, was there the tree of life, which bare twelve manner of fruits, and yielded her fruit every month: and the leaves of the tree were for the healing of the nations. And there shall be no more curse: but the throne of God and of the Lamb shall be in it; and his servants shall serve him: And they shall see his face; and his name shall be in their foreheads. And there shall be no night there; and they need no candle, neither light of the sun; for the Lord God giveth them light: and they shall reign for ever and ever.

Just like these mountain streams that are clear and crisp, this river will flow out of the throne and will be even more pure, perfectly clean. In scripture, water and moving water picture the Holy Spirit. So here we see God the Father, the Son and the Holy Spirit as one. And the tree of life. Notice the size in the street and on either side of the river. I'm not sure, but I believe this is the same tree that was in the Garden of Eden. God would not let Adam and Eve partake of the tree because they would live forever in that sinful state. Now that man is perfect and eternal, he can eat of that fruit.

As the sun sets behind the mountains, darkness begins to cover the forest. The day is done. The sky darkens, and the moon begins to rise in the east. I hear the howl of a lonely coyote off in the distance. Maddie has now finished hunting. She comes by my side, and we walk down the trail toward the truck. I thank the Lord that He has given us an enjoyable day, and I think back on things I should and shouldn't have done as well as what we accomplished. Maddie worked really hard and gave everything she had. I had successes as well as failures, but as I evaluate, I can be thankful for a pretty good day.

Just as every day comes to a close, every life must come to a close. As you look back on your life, what have you accomplished? Before we can know how to leave life, we must first know how to live life. Jesus said, "I am the way the truth and the life." Life is only through Jesus Christ, and without Him, our accomplishments are worthless. I once preached at the funeral of a World War II paratrooper. I used the analogy of the soldier preparing his parachute pack before his jump. During that time, suppose he had loaded his pack with the pleasures of life—money and other things that were precious to him—or maybe had been too busy to prepare at all. After the troops were loaded onto the plane and headed over for battle, the sergeant yelled, "Jump!" With rifle in hand and ready to fight, he jumped into space. He then pulled the cord, and all those things came flying out, but they were worthless. He was so caught up in other things that he forgot the most important of them all, a simple parachute.

We spend much of our lives preparing. As kids, we go to school to prepare for college, and then we go to college to prepare for the workforce. While we are working, we prepare for retirement. While we are preparing for retirement, we prepare for children and their college so they can go to school and prepare, and it goes on and on. Our packs are full, and when we step out into eternity, all these things come out, and we realize we forgot the most important thing, the parachute. Jesus is our parachute. He is the way, the truth, and the life. No man cometh unto the Father but by Him. Truly living life is preparing for eternity here on earth because once you step across that line, there is no turning back. Are you prepared? Have you trusted Him today?

My grandfather, Dr. Chris Harman, lived his life the way he wanted. He devoted his life to the practice of veterinary medicine, and when he wasn't practicing, he was hunting. He was a healthy man so not much slowed him down, even into his eighties, until one morning when I got a phone call. He needed someone to take him to the doctor. He had been bitten by a small deer tick while fox hunting and was almost paralyzed. When I arrived, I literally had to lift him into the car. After a few tests, the doctor diagnosed him with Rocky Mountain spotted fever, but that was only part of it. Granddad had a blood cancer that he had contracted from working with medicines. The cancer had been dormant, but the fever had accelerated the cancer. There was nothing to do but give blood transfusions, and that would only work for a short time. If that wasn't enough, Granddad had a far greater problem than that. Though he was a good man and well thought of in the community, in fact, I would go as far as to say a legend in these parts, he was still a sinner, as lost as he could be and on his way to a Christ-less eternity. I had talked to him about salvation a few times, but he would only get angry and say, "What makes you think your way is right?" I still prayed for him. Over the next year, we all prayed that the Lord would heal him, but we prayed just as much that he would come to Jesus Christ and his soul would be saved. Many preachers visited him and prayed with him, but it seemed to no avail until finally one night I got a call. It was Granddad. He said, "Chris, I want to tell you something." I replied, "What's that, Granddad?" He said, "I got saved today. I trusted Jesus Christ as my Savior." With nowhere else to turn and realizing his time was short, he called for my pastor, Leon Wood, who showed him how to be saved and led him to Jesus. I hung up the phone that night with tears streaming down my face. I stopped and thanked the Lord for answered prayer and His amazing and marvelous grace. Granddad was now ready to step into eternity, and on February 22, 2000, the Lord Jesus Christ welcomed him home.

We continue walking in the dark toward the truck. In the distance I can see the reflection of the moonlight on the windshield. It is comforting to know where I'm going and that safety and rest are not far away. When we near the end of life, it seems like darkness is all around and the day is almost gone, but how comforting it is to know the Lord is with us and His light is shining ahead. We can rejoice knowing we will be in His very presence and see Him face-to-face. To use the words of Paul, "I have fought a good fight. I have finished the course."

As we cross that finish line, we can look forward to seeing our Savior and hearing those long-awaited words, "Well done, thy good and faithful servant. Welcome home."

ABOUT THE AUTHOR

Chris Harman is a Bible teacher of over twenty years at New Haven Baptist Church in Floyd, Virginia. As a third-generation bird hunter, he likes to use his beloved bird dogs and experiences to teach the simple truths of God's word, that many would be saved and better serve the Lord. Chris is also married to his high school sweetheart, Rebecca, and has been blessed with three children.